Judaism in a Nutshell

An Easy-to-Use Guide For People Who Are Long on Curiosity, But Short on Time.

HOLIDAYS

Shimon Apisdorf

Don't miss—Judaism in a Nutshell: GOD

Listen to what people are saying—

This book unravels many of the mysteries and complexities about God, and presents them in easy-to-understand ideas.

David J. Lieberman, Ph.D. Best-selling author, *Never Be Lied To Again*

The ideas are very deep, yet the style is a delight and easy to read. It would be a good idea to reread this book every few years—it's just that important."

Andrew Goldfinger, Ph.D. Assistant Director of the Space Department's Mission Concept and Analysis Group. Author, *Thinking About Creation*

Judaism in a Nutshell: Holidays
by Shimon Apisdorf

Copyright © 2001 Shimon Apisdorf & Judaica Press

Leviathan Press
17 Warren Road Suite 18
Pikesville, Maryland 21208
(410) 653-0300
www.leviathanpress.com

ISBN 1-881927-22-9

Printed in the United States of America
First edition
Cover design by Staiman Design
Page layout by Fisherman Sam and Herzog Design
Technical consultants: E.R./D.L./Y.B.Z./B.C.
Editorial services by Sharon Goldinger/PeopleSpeak

Distributed to the trade by NBN (800) 462-6420
Distributed to Judaica stores by Judaica Press (800) 972-6201

All books from Leviathan Press are available at bulk order
discounts for educational, promotional and fund raising
purposes. For information call (800) 538-4284.
Titles include:

Rosh Hashanah Yom Kippur Survival Kit
One Hour Purim Primer   Remember My Soul
Passover Survival Kit   Survival Kit Family Haggadah
Bible for the Clueless but Curious   Death of Cupid
Missiles, Masks, and Miracles   JUDAISM IN A NUTSHELL: GOD
Chanukah: Eight Nights of Light, Eight Gifts for the Soul

ACKNOWLEDGEMENTS

Rabbi Michel and Rebbetzin Feige Twerski, Michael Monson, Rabbi Menachem Goldberger, Bill Hackney, Yigal Segal, Tobey Herzog, Sharon Auerbach, Brian Appelstein, Tali Katz, Aryeh Mezei, Nachum Shapiro, Stella Rae, and special thanks to Mr. David Baum.

SPECIAL THANKS

My parents, David and Bernice Apisdorf. I, for one, am glad you *didn't* skip parenthood on the way to grandparenthood.

Mr. and Mrs. Robert and Charlotte Rothenburg. May you be blessed with years of health and *nachas*.

Esther Rivka, Ditzah Leah, Yitzchak Ben Zion, and Baruch Chananya. Soon, in Jerusalem.

Miriam. Your love, commitment, and awesome sense of humor transform dreams into reality.

Hakadosh Baruch Hu, source of all blessing.

table of
contents

Introduction   7

1. The Holidays and Their Stories   9
   the jumble of history in a nice little nutshell

2. Holidays, History, and Marriage   33
   a framework for a deeper understanding of the spiritual
   concepts that unify the holidays and history

3. The Nuts and Bolts of the Holidays   55
   a hands-on guide to celebrating the holidays

4. Just When You Thought You Knew It All   73
   a collection of mini-essays exploring new dimensions of
   the holidays

   Epilogue: Simple Complexity   93

   Notes   95

introduction

J ewish holidays are a celebration of the most
profound elements of all existence.

*"What would have happened to the human race if
Abraham had not been a man of great sagacity, or if he
had stayed in Ur and kept his higher notions to himself,
and no specific Jewish people had come into being?
Certainly the world without the Jews would have been a
radically different place."*

Paul Johnson, *A History of the Jews*[1]

Ever since the days of Abraham, Jews have made a career out
of looking at reality in often radically different ways from the rest
of the world. In the course of Jewish life, it is the holidays that
embody the distinctly Jewish view of the world.

This book will deal with what are commonly referred to as
Judaism's "major" holidays. These are the holidays that have
their roots in the Torah—the Five Books of Moses—like Passover
and Yom Kippur, or those that came into existence during the era
of the first and second Jewish commonwealths, like Chanukah
and Purim. The goal of this book is to provide a structure that
will enable you to understand the cycle of the Jewish calendar
and all its major holidays within a framework that represents the

essence of Jewish life. Additionally, if you have little or no familiarity with the holidays or if there are holidays that you have never celebrated but might like to explore, this book will present an outline of the basic information required to take your first foray into the holidays.

The book is divided into four sections. The first section surveys early Jewish history, where we not only look at the historical events related to the holidays, but also see how the holidays are actually ongoing expressions of those events. The second section offers a global perspective of historical events, the holidays, and the underlying spiritual concepts that unify them. The third section presents the practical, hands-on elements that go into the celebration of each holiday. Lastly, the fourth section is a collection of mini-essays that explores alternative pathways of thought that grow out of the holidays. These essays will challenge you to think, and think again, not only about the holidays but about life itself.

Today, many Jews, through no fault of their own, feel like strangers in their own home. They feel that Judaism and Jewish life are a foreign and foreboding domain. While people may identify as Jews, at the same time, they feel uncomfortable and even alienated from their very Jewishness. I know this feeling well. As the saying goes, "Been there, done that."

My hope is that this book will be a portal through which you will discover a connection to Judaism that you may never have thought possible. It is also my hope that after reading this book you will feel at ease, like an insider, with any of the holidays.

I want to extend my deepest thanks to my wife Miriam with whom I have been privileged to celebrate so many wonderful holidays. It is her devotion to Judaism, and to life, that has enabled our home to become a sanctuary for the holidays, for spirituality, and for life.

the holidays and their
Stories

1

The Jumble of History in a Nice Little Nutshell

History, Holidays, and Context

Does the name Joseph ring a bell?

Okay, how about Joseph and the coat of many colors—sound familiar?

If you are familiar with the Biblical personality of Joseph, then you've got the basic context for the historical roots of Passover. If you aren't familiar with Joseph, don't worry about it, because the following chart has been designed specifically with you in mind.

Holiday Continuum: History and Holidays

Exodus from Egypt	Torah given at Sinai	Golden Calf; shattered tablets — Jerusalem besieged	Spies. Jews in desert refuse to enter Israel — Temples I & II are destroyed	Creation. Adam and Eve	God forgives Jews for the Golden Calf, and gives second set of tablets	Divine Clouds protect the Jews in the desert	Revolt against Greece / Flask of oil burns for eight days	Esther and Mordecai save the Jews from Haman
Passover	Shavuot	Seventeenth of Tamuz	Ninth of Av	Rosh Hashanah	Yom Kippur	Sukkot — Shemini Atzeret	Chanukah	Purim
15-21 Nisan	6 Sivan	17 Tamuz	9 Av	1-2 Tishrei	10 Tishrei	15-21 Tishrei — 22 Tishrei	25 Kislev-3 Tevet	14 & 15 Adar
March/April	May/June	June/July	July	September	October	October	December	March

Holiday Stories in a Nutshell

Hopefully, the previous chart and calendar have provided you with a feel for the flow of Jewish history and how the holidays fit into the formative stages of the history of the Jewish people. The following summaries will tell the stories of the major holidays, and after studying them together with the chart and calendar, you will be well on your way to being a certified Jewish nutshell historian.

Passover

It All Starts with Abraham

In the year 2017, God and Abraham cut a deal known as the Covenant. As a part of this covenant, God promised Abraham that He would have a unique relationship with his descendants, that they would grow into a nation that would be a source of blessing for all mankind, and that their place of residence would be a slice of the Middle East called Israel. However, Abraham was also informed that a part of the formative years of this budding covenant would be an experience of national hardship.

> *"And He* [God] *said to Abraham 'You need to know that your descendants will be strangers in a land that is not theirs, and they will be enslaved and oppressed for four hundred years. Eventually, however, I will judge the nation that oppresses them, and then they will leave with great wealth.'"*
>
> Genesis 15:13-14

These words foreshadowed the events that would ultimately lead to the holiday of Passover.

Joseph and Egypt

Abraham had a son named Isaac, Isaac had a son named Jacob, and Jacob had twelve sons (the twelve tribes of Israel), one of whom was Joseph. Jacob and Joseph had a special relationship that was symbolized by an unusually beautiful coat that Jacob gave to Joseph. This special relationship gave rise to a little tension between Joseph and his brothers. The culmination of this uneasy relationship took place when the brothers sold Joseph to a caravan of merchants headed for Egypt and then told their father that he had been killed by a wild animal. Well, a funny thing happened to Joseph in Egypt. Being the bright and capable Jewish kid that he was—and possessing a knack for interpreting dreams—Joseph was eventually appointed to be the Egyptian prime minister and right-hand man to Pharaoh himself.

The Return of the Brothers

A number of years after the sale of Joseph, a devastating famine hit the land of Israel (then known as Canaan) where Jacob, his sons, and their families lived. As luck would have it—based on his interpretation of one of Pharaoh's dreams—the new Prime Minister of Egypt had actually foretold the coming of this very famine. As a result, Egypt had stock-piled plenty of food and was capable not only of providing for itself but also of selling surplus grain to others.

Jacob heard about the grain that was being sold in Egypt and dispatched his sons to make a purchase. And guess whom they had to meet with in order to purchase the food they needed? Their long lost brother Joseph. Though they didn't recognize Joseph, he recognized them and devised a plan to spur them into realizing the mistake they had made.

The Jews Come to Egypt

Joseph's plan worked like a charm. Before long, Jacob was reunited with his long lost son, and the entire family was completing the first Jewish move to the suburbs. In fact, the Jews lived quite comfortably in the suburb of Goshen for many years until (dramatic music, please) matters took a turn for the worse. The Egyptian populace soon forgot how Joseph had saved them, became uncomfortable with how well the Jews were doing in Egypt, and had a new Pharaoh who raised the specter of dual loyalty. Within a short period of time, the Jews were reduced to brutally oppressed slave laborers.

Along Comes Moses

While the Jews were suffering under the yoke of slavery, a baby by the name of Moses happened to be found and adopted by none other than the daughter of Pharaoh himself. After being raised in the palace of Pharaoh and witnessing the hardships imposed upon the people of his birth, Moses decided to assert his identity as a Jew. This search for his roots got Moses in a lot of trouble with the Egyptians, and he was forced to flee the country. Having thrown in his lot with his people and now being on his own, Moses got more than he bargained for. What he got was nothing less than an encounter with God at the burning bush. And instead of getting just a pat on the back for boldly asserting his Jewish identity, Moses was commissioned by God to be His personal representative to Pharaoh. That's right, Moses was being sent back to Egypt to inform Pharaoh that none other than the Creator of the universe had ordered the liberation of the Jews from slavery.

A Twisted Arm

As you can imagine, Pharaoh wasn't all that impressed by Moses' announcement. So God had to do a little arm twisting, and nine plagues later (frogs, locust, hail, and so on), the Jews were almost free. Just one more plague, the death of the firstborn, was needed to break Pharaoh's will and bring about the liberation of the Jewish people from slavery in Egypt. And that's exactly what happened.

Matzah, Anybody?

Following the capitulation of Pharaoh, God led the Jewish people out of Egypt and into the desert. That event, the Exodus from Egypt, took place on the fifteenth day of the Hebrew month of Nisan and has been commemorated ever since at the Passover seder. The Passover seder, with its matzah, four cups of wine, and reading of the Haggadah, is the central element of the Passover holiday and the way that Jewish families have been recounting and reliving the events of the Exodus for the last three thousand years.

The story that began with Abraham and a covenant eventually led to the events surrounding Jacob and his children. The story of Jacob's sons—Joseph and his brothers—evolved into the story of Moses and the Jewish bondage in Egypt, a story that culminated with the birth of a free and independent Jewish people.

Shavuot

The End Is Just the Beginning

While the Exodus was the grand finale of four hundred years of Jewish history, in truth, it was also just the beginning. The next chapter in the story would lead directly from the Egyptian border to the foot of a mountain called Sinai.

Good-bye Egypt, Hello Mount Sinai

The Jewish nation, with Moses as their fearless leader and God's pillar of fire blazing the way, marched out of Egypt and left behind the ruins of a humbled country devastated by the ten plagues. In front of them lay a vast expanse of inhospitable wilderness, a great unknown. But one thing they knew for sure, God was leading them every step of the way. They also knew that they were headed for a remarkable destination, because when Moses first approached Pharaoh he said,

> *"The God of Israel has said, 'You must send out my nation so they can celebrate with me... the God of the Jews has appeared to us; we must travel for three days in the desert where we will bring offerings to God..."*

> Exodus 5:1-3

Hey, Who Put That Sea There?

Just one week after leaving Egypt, with God's pillars of fire and cloud leading them through the wilderness, the Jews found themselves camped at the shore of the Sea of Reeds. Then, just when they were taking bets about how God would circumnavigate this little obstacle, their worst nightmare came true. The Egyptians had a change of heart, Pharaoh successfully rallied his troops, and the Egyptian army was in hot pursuit. If ever there was a rock and a hard place, this was it. The sea was in front of them, the Egyptian army was closing in, and they panicked. But then, just in the nick of time, the sea split, the Jews walked through, and their pursuers were drowned as the sea caved in all around them. Finally, their freedom was complete.

The Road to Shavuot and the Holidays

After catching their collective breath on the other side of the sea, the Jews, still following God's pillars of fire and cloud, continued their trek to Sinai. The trip took another five and a half weeks. At last, on the third day of the month of Sivan, the entire Jewish nation reached their destination: Mount Sinai. At that point they were just three days away from receiving the Torah from God, three days away from what would become the holiday of Shavuot.

In the context of the Jewish holidays, the interim period between the Exodus and the revelation at Sinai is significant for three reasons.

1. The Seventh Day of Passover

The holiday of Passover is celebrated for seven days. The first day is the anniversary of the Exodus, the actual day of liberation, and is well known because of the Passover seder. The seventh day, though it is less famous than the first, marks the anniversary of the splitting of the sea and is understood to be the culmination of the liberation.

2. The Counting of the *Omer*

The entire trip from Egypt to receiving the Torah at Mount Sinai took forty-nine days. These forty-nine days are celebrated through a process known as *sefirat haomer*, the counting of the *omer*. Every year, beginning with the second night of Passover, Jews are commanded to verbally count the forty-nine days from Passover to Shavuot.

3. Shavuot

There exists a curious fact about the holiday of Shavuot. It is the only holiday named for what took place *before* it, as opposed to being named for what actually occurred *on* the holiday. The word *shavuot* means "weeks." The weeks that are being referred to are the seven weeks between Passover and Shavuot. So, while what took place on Shavuot was the giving of the Torah at Mount Sinai (as we will see in a moment), its name is related to what took place *before* the Torah was given. (The meaning of this unique phenomenon will be explored on page 85.)

Shavuot, a Day That Changed All of History

By the time the Jews reached Mount Sinai, they were just three days away from an event that would not only set the course for the rest of Jewish history but would profoundly shape the direction of world history. Once they were comfortably settled in at the foot of the mountain, God told Moses to instruct the Jewish people about how to ready themselves for the most intense experience they would ever have. If you thought the ten plagues and the splitting of the sea were something, these were nothing compared to God's direct communication to the entire nation. Never before—and never since—has an entire nation experienced a direct encounter with the Creator of the universe.

On the sixth day of the month of Sivan, God revealed Himself to the Jewish people and offered them the Torah—and the Jewish people accepted. In many ways, the rest of Jewish history is the story of the relationship of the Jews to the Torah. The first part of the story goes like this:

The Seventeenth of Tamuz

Forty Days Later

After the Jewish people accepted God's offer of the Torah, Moses ascended Mount Sinai, where he would spend forty days studying all of its details. At the conclusion of that forty-day marathon of Torah study, God gave Moses a diploma in the form of two tablets with the Ten Commandments inscribed on them. With these tablets in hand, Moses was ready to head down the mountain, present them to the nation and begin teaching the people everything he had learned. But things didn't exactly go according to plan.

Hey, Moses, How Do You Like Our Golden Calf?

When Moses came down from the mountain, he was shocked by the sight that greeted him. While he was away, the people had built a golden calf as an object of worship. To say the least, Moses was stunned and knew of no other way to respond than to smash the precious tablets he had so eagerly looked forward to giving to the people.

The day on which the tablets were smashed was the seventeenth day of the month of Tamuz. From that time on, the Seventeenth of Tamuz, a day that was slated for joy and celebration, became a day of deep sadness. Centuries later, the tragedy of the Seventeenth of Tamuz would echo once again in Jewish history when the walls of Jerusalem were breached on that day, prior to the destruction of the Temple.

To this day, the Seventeenth of Tamuz is observed as a day of fasting and is the first day of a period known as the Three Weeks. The Three Weeks is a period of progressive mourning that begins with the Fast of the Seventeenth of Tamuz and concludes with the Ninth of Av, the day of greatest Jewish tragedy and mourning. (We'll take a closer look at the Ninth of Av soon.)

The High Holidays

Yom Kippur, Aftermath of the Calf

One of the concepts that Moses learned about while he was on Mount Sinai was the High Holidays, the days of Rosh Hashanah and Yom Kippur. Rosh Hashanah is the Jewish New Year's Day (more about that later), and Yom Kippur is a day for owning up to one's mistakes to God and receiving atonement. Little did Moses realize, but Yom Kippur, the day of forgiveness and atonement, was about to come in very handy.

The Two Tablets: Let's Try That One Again

After his stay on the mountain ended in bitter disappointment, Moses spent the next forty days acting as a sort of spiritual arbitrator between God and the Jewish people. At the end of that forty-day reconciliation period, God invited Moses back up the mountain for another try. This time, things went better.

Moses' second stint at the top of Mount Sinai—another forty-day process—began on the first day of the month of Elul, the last month of the Jewish calendar year. Moses' stay lasted throughout the entire month of Elul and into Tishrei, the first month of the year. The last ten days that Moses was on the mountain included Rosh Hashanah, the first day of Tishrei, and Yom Kippur, the tenth of Tishrei. As it turned out, Moses came down from the mountain with the second set of tablets on Yom Kippur, the day of atonement and forgiveness.

Sukkot

A Little Background

The central feature of the holiday of Sukkot is the *sukkah*, or temporary booth, that people build and live in for the week of the holiday. The question is, why? Why do we build and move into these temporary, makeshift dwellings throughout the holiday of

Sukkot? The answer is that these dwellings are meant to recall the portable shelters that the Jewish people lived in during their travels in the desert as well as the divine protection that was with them at that time. According to our tradition, there was a dual dimension to the shelter that the Jews had in the desert. On the one hand, they had these portable structures that they lived in while they were there. At the same time, they benefited from the shelter and guidance that was provided by God's protective clouds—known as the Divine Clouds of Glory—that traveled with them wherever they went. These protective clouds were an ever-present symbol that the Jews were secure in God's hands. He was with them at the Exodus, with them at Mount Sinai, and continued to be with them throughout their journey to the promised land of Israel.

And now, back to history.

Today's Forecast: Mostly Cloudy with More on the Way

If you've ever wondered where all those Jews lived when they marched out of Egypt, now you know. As soon as the Jews left Egypt, they set up makeshift huts and were surrounded by the Divine Clouds of Glory. And that felt great. In fact, according to the sages, nothing was more joyous than the feeling of being sheltered by God.

Unfortunately, there was a period of time when the clouds parted and the skies above the Jewish people cleared up, which, in this case, was not a good sign. You'll recall that on the seventeenth of Tamuz the Jews built a golden calf that prompted Moses' smashing of the tablets. Well, those broken tablets weren't the only response to the calf. God also responded, and His response was the removal of the Divine Clouds.

The absence of the Divine Clouds lasted for a few months. During the time that Moses was trying to patch things up between God and the Jewish people, the clouds stayed away. While Moses was back on the mountain, the clouds were still away. Not until five days after Yom Kippur, five days after Moses came down with the second set of tablets, did the clouds return.

The date of their return was the fifteenth of Tishrei, which just happens to be the first day of the holiday of Sukkot.

Things Are Looking Pretty Good

Let's take a moment to review the history and the holidays we have just described.

The first major historical event was the Exodus from Egypt, which was a good thing and is commemorated by the holiday of Passover. From there we moved to Mount Sinai and the giving of the Torah, also a good thing, and that event is marked by the holiday of Shavuot. From there, we went to the building of the golden calf, the smashing of the tablets, and the removal of the clouds—definitely not good things—all of which are remembered through the fast of the Seventeenth of Tamuz. Then, just as everything was looking bleak, events started to swing back in a good direction. By Rosh Hashanah, God and the Jews were well on their way to reconciliation; by Yom Kippur, the broken tablets had been replaced with a brand new pair; by Sukkot, the clouds were back and a state of joy had returned to the Jewish nation. Now, back to our story.

Welcome to the Tabernacle

After the clouds returned on Sukkot, the situation of the Jews in the desert went from good to better. When Moses came down from Mount Sinai, in addition to the new tablets, he had other great news. God wanted the Jews to build a very special structure that would be a place where His Presence would constantly be manifest among the people. While it was true that the Divine Clouds in the desert provided an ever-present awareness of God's closeness to the nation, these clouds were only temporary and would disappear once the Jews entered the land of Israel. In their place, God told the people to build a Tabernacle (the Hebrew word is *mishkan*, which means "a dwelling place"). This Tabernacle would include such things as the Menorah (a spectacular golden candelabra), the Ark of the Covenant (remember Indiana Jones) that had the Torah in it, and a number of other items all designed to foster and maintain the closeness between God and the Jews that the clouds represented. Eventually, once the people became settled and secure in Israel, the Tabernacle took its permanent form as the Temple in Jerusalem.

The Ninth of Av

Next Stop, Israel

For the next seven months, the Jews remained camped at the foot of Mount Sinai and focused all their energies on the construction of the Tabernacle. By the spring, just before Passover, the job was finished. From God's perspective, the completion of the Tabernacle set the stage for the Jews to travel on to the land of Israel, but that's where the situation got dicey again.

Maybe We Should Check This Place Out First

Basically, the Jews got cold feet. Just as they were about to break camp and head for the Promised Land, the people decided that it might be a good idea to send an advance group of spies to scout out the land. Moses, sensing the people's waning enthusiasm for Israel, begrudgingly consented to their idea. From that point on, it was all downhill.

Moses appointed a group of spies and sent them on a mission to check out the land of Israel and return with a full report—hopefully an upbeat and glowing one. Unfortunately, their report was less than glowing and the reaction of the people was even worse. Their response went something like, "We're not going. We don't care how great you say it is. We're not, we're not, we're not!" And then they began to cry. And how did God respond to this? His response went something like this, "Look, if you don't want to go, I'm not going to force you." And for the next thirty-eight years the Jews wandered through the desert until that generation passed away and a new one matured that *did* want to settle in Israel.

That night, the night that the Jewish people cried and spurned the land of Israel, was the ninth day of the month of Av. Much later in history, that same date would become the date on which the Temple in Jerusalem was destroyed.

The Land of Israel, Jerusalem, and the Temple

The land of Israel is much more than a quaint Jewish suburb in a predominantly Arab neighborhood; the land of Israel is where the Jewish people and God were destined to live together. The seeds of a relationship between God and the Jewish people that had been planted in the desert were meant to take root and blossom in Israel, the land originally promised to Abraham. And the heart of all of Israel was to be the Temple in Jerusalem. So when the Jews turned their backs on Israel, they were actually turning their backs on God.

The Three Weeks

You'll recall that the debacle of the golden calf took place on the seventeenth of Tamuz. Look at our calendar and you will see that it's just three weeks from the seventeenth of Tamuz until the ninth of Av. Considering what happened on those dates in the desert—and later in Jewish history—it's no wonder that the Three Weeks mark a period of extended mourning that begins on the seventeenth of Tamuz and builds to a bitter crescendo on the ninth of Av.

Let's Review

Before we go any further, let's think about the holidays we've discussed so far and the ones we haven't. Of the six biblical holidays, Passover, Shavuot, Sukkot, Shemini Atzeret, Rosh Hashanah, and Yom Kippur, we have touched on all but one, Shemini Atzeret. We'll get to that one later on page 40. Of the four major holidays from the postbiblical era, we have touched on two, the Seventeenth of Tamuz and the Ninth of Av. The other two major rabbinical, or postbiblical holidays, Chanukah and Purim, are what we are about to look at. Here goes.

Purim

No Roots Here

All of the holidays we have seen until now have a direct relationship to early Jewish history as it is presented in the Torah. Even the Seventeenth of Tamuz, the Three Weeks, and the Ninth of Av, though they weren't enacted as holidays until many centuries after the end of the biblical period, have clear roots in the events of the Torah. Purim and Chanukah are different. On the surface, they have no apparent relationship to events in the Torah, and each stands on its own as a singular event in later Jewish history. Let's take a look.

Forty Years in the Desert, Seven Hundred in Israel

Though the trip took a little longer than was originally planned, the Jews finally made it to the land of Israel. The setting-up-shop process took three hundred and fifty years (remember, this was before the United Jewish Appeal, Israel Bonds, and heavy construction equipment) and was concluded when the Tabernacle took its permanent form as King Solomon's Temple in Jerusalem. For the next four hundred years, a vibrant Jewish community flourished in the land of Israel, with Jerusalem and the Temple as its spiritual, cultural, and political center.

Then, as today, the Near Eastern world surrounding Israel was a hotbed of geopolitical activity. Empires in Egypt, Assyria, and Babylonia vied for power and prestige. Eventually the Babylonians, with Nebuchadnezzar as their king, became the pre-eminent regional power. This regional superpower, headed by Nebuchadnezzar, conquered Jerusalem and destroyed the Temple some four hundred years after it was built.

The destruction of Jerusalem ushered in the period of Jewish history known as the Babylonian exile. The Jews who survived the Babylonian onslaught were taken in humiliation to Babylon. Over time, they were able to build a vibrant Jewish community and were, to a great degree, afforded the ability to conduct their religious and communal lives with a good deal of social independence.

Some fifty years after the expulsion from Israel, Babylonia fell to the Persians. Having been slaves in Egypt, sovereign in Israel, and then exiled by the Babylonians, the Jews were now subject to the rule of one of the greatest empires ever to appear on the stage of history—that of the Persians. It would be that empire and its rulers, Cyrus and his successor Achashverosh, who would provide the stage and setting upon which the story of Purim would take place.

Haman—Boo; Mordecai and Esther—Hooray!

The story of Purim, as told in the Book of Esther, is the firsthand account of a turn of events that constituted a dramatic reversal of fortune for the Jewish people. Like all good stories, the Book of Esther is a tale of good guys versus bad guys. The good guys are Esther and Mordecai—the heroes responsible for saving the Jews from a genocidal decree. The bad guys are King Achashverosh and Haman. Haman was a man whose hatred for the Jewish people fueled his meteoric rise to power in the court of King Achashverosh and who sought to use the leverage of his position to bring about the extermination of the Jewish people. In the end, it was a combination of Mordecai's wisdom, Esther's courage, and God's behind-the-scenes orchestration that saved the Jews from the closing jaws of a hate-driven leadership and an all-too-willing population of accomplices.

The Story of Purim in a Nutshell

Scene I.

King Achashverosh throws the party of the century, a one-hundred-and-eighty-seven day bash celebrating the third year of his reign. Sometime during the festivities, Achashverosh requests that Queen Vashti appear unclothed before his guests. An indignant Vashti refuses the king's request, is summarily deposed as queen, and then, after a lengthy search for a new queen, is replaced by a woman named Esther. Unbeknownst to the king, Esther is a Jew.

Scene II.

Haman is appointed Prime Minister of the Persian empire and uses his newfound power to initiate a royal decree granting citizens the freedom to slaughter their Jewish neighbors. Achashverosh signs the decree. Jumping into action, Esther's uncle, a leading Jewish sage by the name of Mordecai, sends a message to Esther saying that the time has come for her to reveal her identity and intervene on behalf of her people. A nervous and hesitant Esther accepts her mission.

Scene III.

Esther invites the king and Haman to a private little party of her own, and Haman can barely contain his glee at being the lone guest at this most exclusive royal affair. (Boy, is he in for a surprise!) At just the right moment, Esther deftly plays her hand, reveals the truth of her identity, fingers Haman as the would-be henchman of her people, and wins the king's favor. Esther's interceding leads to the execution of Haman and a second royal decree enabling the Jews to be saved.

Scene IV.

The fourteenth and fifteenth days of the Hebrew month of Adar are designated as a holiday commemorating this miraculous turn of events. From then on, these days are celebrated as the holiday of Purim.

Chanukah

Time for a Second Temple

Not long after the events of Purim, Darius, the new Persian king and the son of Achashverosh and Esther, allowed the Jews to return to Jerusalem and rebuild the Temple. Though still under the aegis of Persia, once again a large Jewish community flourished in Israel. Jerusalem and the Temple were its heart and soul.

While the Jews were re-establishing themselves in Israel, just on the horizon of history, a new empire—Greece—was beginning to make its presence felt. Less than thirty years after the rebuilding of the Temple, Alexander the Great became the greatest conqueror the world had ever known. It wasn't long until Persia was defeated and Israel fell under Greek domination.

From Athens to Atlanta

Over two thousand five hundred years ago, the great Greek god Zeus set up shop on Mount Olympus. In honor of this mighty deity and the dynasty of gods he headed, a spectacular sporting event was launched at the village of Olympia. Today, cities like Atlanta, Sydney, and Seoul vie for the honor of carrying on the grand tradition of the Olympic games.

Olympic competition is just one example of the far-reaching influence that Hellenism, the culture of Greece, had on the world. It was the Greeks, and after them the Romans (Roman culture was an extension of Greek culture), who brought philosophy, the study of history, athletic competition, sophisticated literature, poetry, a well-developed theater, architecture, urban planning, and the concept of democracy to Europe and eventually, by extension, to America.

> *"We ourselves, whether we like it or not, are the heirs of the Greeks and the Romans. In a thousand different ways, they are permanently and indestructibly woven into the fabric of our own existence."*
>
> Michael Grant, *The Founders of the Western World* [2]

The Jews Resist Hellenism

Not until the rise of McDonald's and Levi's Jeans would another culture even come close to the worldwide influence that

Hellenism had. While the rest of the world tried to resist the powerful Greek forces, once subdued they put up little resistance to Greek culture. When it came to the Jews, just the opposite was true. Though they put up no fight against Alexander's army, when it came to Hellenism, the cultural glory of Greece, most Jews had one response: resistance. The question is, why? The Jewish people were a people who revered education, literacy, and deep thinking. In this regard, the Greeks should have been their soul mates, another enlightened people in an otherwise illiterate and barbarous world. This was not, however, how the Jews saw the issue.

So What Were the Jews So Bothered About?

There was much about Greek culture that, as attractive as it was, was anathema to the Jews. One clash revolved around morality and the sanctity of human life. For all its beauty, Greek society contained prominent aspects that would be absolutely abhorrent to most people today, and were certainly abhorrent to the Jews of two thousand years ago. In Greek society, babies were routinely placed in clay jars and left to die from exposure for the crime of being ugly or deformed, for being sickly, or for being one too many heirs among whom a father could divide his estate. Right behind infanticide on the list of what we today consider deviant behavior was pederasty. We call it child molesting. For us, it is virtually impossible to imagine that the great minds of Greece created a "philosophy" that justified, and even glorified, the man-boy relationship. But that is exactly what happened. In Greece there was a general understanding that the highest and purest form of love was something *we* consider the most heinous of crimes.

The Jewish people are, and even two thousand years ago were, a people who placed the utmost value on human life and who considered the relationship between husband and wife, and parents and children, to be holy. Such a people just couldn't tolerate a society that advocate infanticide and pedophilia, as well as the advocating of adultery and institutionalized prostitution. But there was more.

The Greeks and the Jews had a fundamentally different view of life. It goes without saying that the Jews looked at the Greek pantheon of gods—gods who drank to excess and came down from Olympus to chase pretty little girls—as nothing more than primitive paganism, but the problem went much deeper than that. It went to the heart of Greek philosophy. In a nutshell, the Greeks saw the human mind as the ultimate tool to fathom the will of nature and from there to build an ideal notion of values and life. The Jews see the human mind as a gift to use to fathom the will of the Creator and from there to build a life of value. One world-view is nature-and man-centered, and the other is God-centered. And that's a world of difference.

Assimilation

Despite the fact that in many ways Hellenism and Judaism were at seemingly irreconcilable odds with one another, powerful political and social forces were at work that made Hellenism appealing to many Jews. First, the only way for a Jew to make social or political inroads was to adopt Greek culture. Second, the Greek world of the theater, the gymnasium, and the symposium (fine dining affairs where men were attended to by beautiful women) presented Jews with appealing attractions unlike any they had ever seen. And last, as repugnant as much of Greek life was, here was a people that, like the Jews, revered education, literacy, and philosophical speculation. With time, many Jews came to see Greek culture as the way of the future and the only path to scaling the heights of social, financial, and political success.

Oppression

Though the great majority of Jews remained loyal to the Torah and Judaism, the rise of a large bloc of Hellenistic Jews inevitably led to internal Jewish struggles. The year 199 BCE was a turning point. Twenty-four years earlier, following the death of Alexander, the Greek empire had been divided among its foremost generals. In 199 BCE, the Seleucid Greek dynasty that ruled from Syria assumed control of Israel. It was under the Seleucids that harsh decrees were issued against the practice of Judaism. All Jews were required to follow the lead of their assimilated Hellenist brethren and embrace Greek culture. It was at that time that the study of Torah and the observance of Judaism brought with them the risk of death.

Revolt

Jerusalem, the spiritual heart of the nation, with its Temple, great Torah academies, and large Jewish population, was the natural target for the fiercest enforcement of the anti-Jewish decrees. It was this intense hounding of the thoroughly loyalist Jews that led Mattisyahu, the scholarly scion of the Hasmonean family, to move his family out of Jerusalem to Modiin. But the reign of terror followed them there, too.

One day, the Greek forces arrived in Modiin and insisted that the Jews offer a sacrifice to a pagan god. Mattisyahu, as a respected elder, was singled out to be an example for the other townspeople, but Mattisyahu was defiant. Mattisyahu refused to be intimidated, but while he stood strong another Jew stepped forward to offer the sacrifice. An enraged Mattisyahu grabbed a sword, killed the renegade Jew and then turned on the Greek soldiers. Soon the small band of Greek soldiers lay dead on the ground in Modiin. The Jewish revolt had begun.

The elderly Mattisyahu died within a year and never saw the success of the revolt he began. After the passing of Mattisyahu, his son Judah took over as leader of the family and of the revolt. A brilliant tactician and leader, Judah organized a fighting force known as the Maccabees. It was under the inspired leadership of Judah Maccabee that the Jews were able to successfully confront the Greeks and eventually recapture the Temple. When the victorious Jewish forces entered the Temple, they found one small flask with enough oil to kindle the great Menorah for just one day. And then a miracle happened; one day's supply of oil continued to burn for eight days.

The rest of the story, as they say, is history.

Next Stop: The Soul

Congratulations. Having completed this section, you are now a member in good standing of the Royal Society of Nutshell Historians. However, lest you be tempted to rest on your laurels, we will now forge ahead—not into more history—but into the metahistory of the holidays, the soul of Jewish history.

It is basic to classical Jewish thought that history is more than just history, and holidays are more than just holidays.

The Fabric of Time

"...the theory of relativity put an end to the idea of absolute time! We must accept that time is not completely separate from and independent of space, but it is combined with it to form an object called space-time."

Stephen W. Hawking, *A Brief History of Time* [3]

"But what happens to space if a massive object like the sun is present? Before Einstein the answer was nothing; space (and time) were thought to provide an inert theater, merely setting the stage on which the events of the universe play themselves out. The chain of Einstein's reasoning that we have been following, however, leads to a different conclusion... to the remarkable suggestion that the presence of mass, such as the sun, causes the fabric of space around it to warp. According to this radical proposal, space is not merely a passive forum providing the arena for the events of the universe; rather, the shape of space [space-time] responds to objects in the universe."

Brian Greene, *The Elegant Universe* [4]

Until Einstein, everyone conceived of life as a series of events unfolding within the context of space and time. Where once space and time were the solid wood floor of the stage, Einstein transformed the stage floor into something that more resembled a taut but malleable surface. Actions no longer passed through time; they actually made impressions upon the very "fabric" of time.

This organic notion of time was a revelation to everyone except the Jews. For centuries, and even millennia before the theory of relativity, the Jewish understanding of time was one that included the potential for events to have a shaping impact on time and in turn, for time to exert an influence on events. This notion goes to the heart of a deeper, spiritual understanding of time, history, and the holidays.

Holidays and the Fabric of Jewish Time

> *"Blessed are You God, our God, sovereign of the universe, who performed miracles for our forefathers, in those days, in this time."*
>
> Chanukah and Purim prayer

There is a large, beautiful tree in front of our house. Like all trees, its vast system of roots is buried beneath the ground. A few large roots, however, are exposed for all to see.

Like our tree, every holiday has two dimensions to its root system—one visible and another less so. The most apparent roots are historical events. These historical roots are what are referred to in the above prayer by the words "in *those* days." Passover is rooted in the Exodus, Purim in the narrow escape from Haman's genocidal plans, and so on. But a deeper and less apparent part of the root system also exists. This is alluded to by the words "in *this* time." Every holiday is rooted both in the events of a specific historical period—"those days"—as well as in the metahistorical fabric of time—"in this time." So, when we celebrate a holiday, we not only recall events that took place in the distant past, we simultaneously come into contact with that same dimension of time—a dimension imbued by events with intrinsic spiritual energies and qualities.

This perspective is essential to fully understanding the holidays, and for actualizing the great potential that each holiday possesses. Far more than history lessons, every Jewish holiday is a fantastic opportunity for spiritual insight, growth, and inspiration.

We will now take a look at this other, deeper dimension of the holidays.

holidays, history, and
Marriage

2

A Framework for a Deeper Understanding

Everybody Is into Holidays

In Japan, February 3 marks the Setsubun bean-throwing festival. April 8 is Buddha's birthday in Korea, September 28 is Confucius's birthday in Taiwan, and October 19 is Ascension of Mohammed Day in Indonesia. Independence Day is May 14 in Paraguay, March 25 in Greece, April 31 in Trinidad and Tobago, and July 4 in the United States. And what self-respecting list of holidays would be complete without Bastille Day, Soweto Day, Kwanzaa, Passover, and Easter?

The very concept of a holiday seems to touch a basic, universal chord. After all, everybody is into them. If you were to show ten people the above list and ask the question, "What's a holiday?" most would probably tell you that they are cultural or religious days that are designated to commemorate something significant in that particular religion or society. And by-and-large they would be correct, with one exception: Passover.

In the Jewish concept, while holidays may appear to be commemorations of historical events, in fact they are something altogether different. The Hebrew word the Torah uses for holiday is *moed*, and *moed* means "rendezvous." Every *moed*, every Jewish holiday, is a meeting of sorts. In fact, Jewish holidays are multidimensional meetings. Think of a business meeting for a moment. Imagine that you have plans to meet with someone at 2:30 on July 24 (Simon Bolivar's birthday in Ecuador) at your seventh floor office on the corner of Twelfth and Main. Is this not a multidimensional meeting? It is taking place within the three dimensions of space, as indicated by the location of your building and the floor your office is on, as well as within the dimension of time, as indicated by the date and hour of the meeting. Additionally, and most importantly, there is a human dimension to your meeting in that what will transpire is two people relating and interacting with one another. In a sense, this is what *moed* is all about.

Jewish holidays are rendezvous that incorporate not only the dimensions of time and place but spiritual dimensions that go to the heart of the Jewish understanding of matters like history, the soul, God, and what it means to be a Jew. To appreciate the depth and import of these holiday-rendezvous events, it is necessary to first take a look at some of the primary components that all converge to form the experiential framework of what we are used to calling holidays but as we will see are actually *moed*, points of rendezvous that bring us to the threshold of the deepest aspects of our existence. Let's take a look—

Rendezvous with Whom?

Well, with God, who else?

Perhaps the most seminal Jewish perspective on God, and one that shapes the entirety of how Jews relate to God in general and the holidays in particular, is this: Since God is wholly complete and lacks nothing, it can't be that His act of creation was motivated by a need, because a need implies a lack, and He has no lackings. Creation, then, is not *for* the Creator, rather, it is *for* us, His creations. If creation is *for* us, what this implies is that existence is for our benefit; in other words, existence is good for us. And, since when God does things He does them right, Judaism understands that the entire purpose of our existence is that we enjoy being able to receive and partake of the greatest good possible. The key words in all of this are "enjoy" and "good." Consequently, God's relationship to us is one in which He is the giver par excellence, and we are the receivers of the best He has to offer. And just what is this "best" that we were created to enjoy? It's the Creator Himself. Therefore, what flows from this is the Jewish perspective that the way we partake in the purpose of what we were created for is to be engaged in a relationship with God. And it is with this perspective that we can gain a comprehensive understanding of the Jewish holidays.

A full appreciation of the holidays begins with understanding them in the context of the relationship between God and the Jewish people. In a word, the relationship between God and the Jewish people is a marriage. This means that the unique depth, intimacy, love, and bonding that is present in marriage provides the best possible analogy for the spiritual connection that is present in the relationship between God and the Jewish people. In fact, King Solomon's *Song of Songs*, a deeply passionate and poignant tribute to the longing and love of a husband and wife, is understood to be an allegory for the love between God and the Jewish nation. It is also regarded as the holiest of all the books of the Bible.

> *"On Passover, Shavuot, and Sukkot* [the three holidays when the Jews visited the Temple in Jerusalem] *the curtain was opened so the people could see the two Cherubs on the Ark of the Covenant embracing. It was then announced to the people, 'God's love for you is like the love of a man and a woman.'"*
>
> Talmud

From the vantage point of seeing God and the Jewish people as lovers, and with the appreciation that the holidays are in fact rendezvous points of love, we will now take a closer look at the Jewish idea of marriage and how it relates to the holidays.

A Word about Marriage

I have been asked the following question on numerous occasions: "If two people live together for many long and happy years, have children together and raise them in a warm and loving home but choose to never formalize their relationship through marriage, are they really any different from another couple who *did* happen to have a wedding?" And what I tell people is this: The Jewish understanding of marriage is that it is a relationship that transcends both the physical, day-to-day practicalities of living together as well as the deep, emotional reality that is a part of building a life, a home, and a family together. Beyond the physical and beyond even the emotional, there is a profound spiritual dimension to marriage. When two people get married, more is taking place than just the first part of sharing a life together; marriage is a spiritual transformation. The souls of two people who marry become blended together as one.

"Therefore a man will leave his mother and father and cleave to his wife and they will become one flesh."

Genesis 2:24

When the Torah speaks about two people becoming "one flesh," it means that marriage is a metamorphosis of essential identity; it is the shift from one's essence being perceived in terms of "I" and "mine" to "us" and "ours" in the deepest and most actual way. It is in the realm of the soul—of the ultimate reality of two people's being—that Judaism sees the difference between a married couple and an equally fulfilled and happy unmarried couple. The marriage ceremony, then, is a sort of re-engineering of two people's spiritual DNA. It is the vehicle through which a new spiritual reality is brought into being—and the only way to describe this new reality is *oneness*. Where once there were two, a wedding now creates one.

Weddings and Holidays

If you have ever been to a Jewish wedding, then you have seen some or all of the following: the bride and the groom stood together under the wedding canopy (the *chuppah*), the rabbi said some prayers, a marriage certificate (the *ketubah*) was read, a ring or rings were exchanged, a glass was broken, and a great party ensued.

I want to let you in on a few secrets.

Secret number one, as we have begun to see, is that the marriage ceremony is more than just a ritual. It's a spiritual process in which each component has its own role, identity, and profound significance. Secret number two is that these component parts of the marriage ceremony have conceptual counterparts in the yearly cycle of the Jewish holidays. And secret number three is that when taken together in the context of early Jewish history, a wedding-holiday paradigm emerges that enables us to understand the holidays on a plane very different from what we are accustomed to. The Jewish holidays, it turns out, are far more than the commemorations of significant historical events. Rather, they are the metahistory of the relationship between God and the Jewish people, and contained within this metahistory are the keys to accessing the great potential of that relationship.

> *"The period of the patriarchs and matriarchs* [Abraham, Sarah, and so on] *was like the courtship and engagement that was followed by the Exodus and the giving of the Torah, which was the wedding."*
>
> Commentary of Malbim, Jeremiah 2:2

> *"The day when the Torah was given at Sinai was the wedding day of God and the Jewish nation."*
>
> Commentary of Rashi and Tsror Hamor, Song of Songs 3:11

> *"God became wedded to the Jewish people at the time of the Exodus and through the giving of the Torah. The consummation took place when God's presence enveloped them."*
>
> Commentary of Eliezer Rokeach, Talmud, Kiddushin

The key to understanding the Jewish holidays lies in being able to see beneath the surface and understand them as a framework for the most transcendent of all relationships: the relationship between the Creator of the universe and the nation of Israel. (For a discussion on the origins, development, and meaning of this relationship see *Judaism in a Nutshell: God.*)

Prologue: Biblical and Postbiblical Holidays

The major holidays can be divided into two general categories: those that are legislated by the Torah (also known as the Bible or the Five Books of Moses) and those that were enacted by the sages of the early postbiblical era. The biblical era is the period dealt with in the Torah itself. This period spans the time from Creation until the death of Moses in 1272 BCE. These years include everything from Adam and Eve to the life of Abraham and Sarah, slavery of the Jews in Egypt, forty years of Jewish wandering in the desert, and a whole lot in between. The early postbiblical era spans the years from the entry of the Jewish people into Israel in 1272 BCE until the destruction of the second Temple by the Romans in the year 70 CE.

Before reading further, take a moment to study the chart on the next page. This overview of Jewish history is designed to give you a sense of the relationship between history and the holidays.

As you can see, there are six holidays whose source is in the Torah—Rosh Hashanah, Passover, Shavuot, Yom Kippur, Sukkot, and Shemini Atzeret—and four that originated in the postbiblical era; the Seventeenth of Tamuz, the Ninth of Av, Purim, and Chanukah. The question is, what if any differences are there between these two groups of holidays? The answer is that there are a number of significant differences, though we will only focus on one central thematic difference. As we will soon see, the conceptual difference that we will explore relates to the idea of exile, and its place and meaning in Jewish history. For now, however, we will begin with the holidays that are enumerated in the Torah itself.

OVERVIEW
JEWISH HISTORY & THE HOLIDAYS

Biblical

Creation / Adam and Eve . . . . 0/3760 BCE
Rosh Hashanah

Abraham and Sarah. 2080/1671 BCE
Egyptian slavery begins . . . . 2332/1428 BCE
Exodus from Egypt . . . . 2448/1312 BCE
Passover

Torah at Mount Sinai. . . . . 2448/1312 BCE
Shavuot

Golden calf / broken tablets. . . . . 2448/1312 BCE
(Seventeenth of Tamuz)
Second tablets / Divine clouds. . . . . 2449/1311 BCE
Yom Kippur
Sukkot
Shemini Atzeret

Spies / rejection of Israel. . . . . 2449/1311 BCE
(Ninth of Av)

Postbiblical

Joshua / Jews enter Israel. . . . . 2488/1272 BCE
First Temple built. . . . . 2935/825 BCE
Jerusalem under siege. . . . . 3338/422 BCE
Seventeenth of Tamuz

Babylonians destroy first Temple. . . . . 3338/422 BCE
Ninth of Av

Persia conquers Babylonia . . . . 3388/372 BCE
Haman is Persian prime minister. . . . . 3404/356 BCE
Esther becomes Queen of Persia. . . . . 3404/356 BCE
Purim

Second Temple built . . . . 3408/352 BCE
Alexander the Great / Greece . . . . 3424/336 BCE
Maccabees / revolt against Greece. . . . . 3596/165 BCE
Temple rededicated / oil burns eight days . . 3597/164 BCE
Chanukah

Romans destroy second Temple. . . . . 3830/70 CE
Ninth of Av

The Marriage-Holiday Paradigm

We are now ready to embark on a five-stage exploration of the marriage-holiday paradigm that will give us a deeper and broader understanding of the concept of holidays as *moed*— rendezvous points of love. The five stages are as follows:

Stage I:	Passover, Shavuot, and Sukkot
Stage II:	Rosh Hashanah and Yom Kippur
Stage III:	Chanukah, Purim, the Three Weeks, and the Ninth of Av
Interlude:	Exile and Redemption
Stage IV:	The Holidays of Exile
Stage V:	The Final Framework

Stage I. Passover, Shavuot, and Sukkot

Will You Marry Me?

In this first stage, we will focus on the three holidays that are classically referred to as the *Shalosh Regalim* or the Three Pilgrimage Festivals. These three festivals are Passover, the festival related to the Exodus from Egypt; Shavuot, the festival connected to God's giving of the Torah on Mount Sinai; and Sukkot, the festival related to the divine protection that accompanied the Jews during their forty years in the desert. These are known as pilgrimage festivals because Jews were obligated to visit the great Temple in Jerusalem during each of these three holidays.

In actuality, there is a fourth holiday that is a part of this group. This is the little known and even less understood holiday of Shemini Atzeret. Though Shemini Atzeret is not officially one of the three festivals, it is closely linked to them because it takes place the day after Sukkot ends. The practical effect of this juxtaposition was that, during the Temple era, when hundreds of thousands of people converged on Jerusalem for Sukkot, they ended up remaining in Jerusalem for an extra day to celebrate

Shemini Atzeret. We will see later that Shemini Atzeret, while it may appear to be almost an afterthought tagged on to the conclusion of Sukkot, is actually the pinnacle of the entire annual cycle of holidays.

In the context of the relationship between God and the Jewish nation, these festivals form the cornerstone of the relationship.

> *"This is analogous to the way in which a man and a woman become connected to one another... like the Talmud says, 'The Jews in the desert* [following the Exodus] *were like an engaged woman and afterwards* [following Sinai] *they were like a married woman.'"*
>
> Commentary of the Netziv, Exodus 19:4

> *"In the larger sense, this is the meaning of the holiday of Sukkot, the holiday of joy... this corresponds to the relationship* [of God to the Jewish people] *that is depicted as the time when the king brings his bride into his private quarters."*
>
> Rabbi Shalom Noach Berzovski, *Paths of Peace* [5]

On Passover, at the time of the Exodus, it was as if God stretched out His hand to His beloved and invited her to follow Him into the desert. According to our tradition, the Jews' decision to follow God was anything but a foregone conclusion; rather, it represented a pivotal first step in the Jewish people's deep commitment to God. In fact, much later in Jewish history, God would look back at that timeless moment and say—

> *"I want to remind you of the kindness of your youth, the way in which you followed Me into the wilderness."*
>
> Jeremiah 2:2

From Egypt to Sinai and Beyond

The journey from the Exodus to the foot of Mount Sinai involved more than just traveling from one place to another. It was the next step in the blossoming of a relationship, a relationship whose new heights would forever be celebrated as the holiday of Shavuot. Every step along the way to Shavuot added new depth to a bond that became more actual when God finally presented, and the Jewish people accepted, the Torah. Then, following the giving of the Torah, came the embrace of ultimate intimacy—God's clouds. The Divine Clouds that enveloped the Jewish nation were an intense manifestation of God's presence and the intimacy that had been realized by lover and beloved. To this very day, we build a *sukkah* to represent those enveloping clouds of intimacy, and we enjoy the feeling of God's embrace. Then, as Sukkot draws to a close, just as we are about to say farewell to the last of the Three Festivals, God says—

> *"I can't bear your leaving, please stay with me just a little longer."*
>
> Rashi, Leviticus 23:36

And so we do. We stay for one more bliss-filled day, Shemini Atzeret, a moment of closeness that transcends all others.

Stage II. Rosh Hashanah and Yom Kippur

Love and Judgment

Rosh Hashanah and Yom Kippur are collectively known as the High Holidays or the Days of Awe. So what is it about these days that make these lofty labels so fitting? What exactly is it that is *so* high and *so* awesome about these days?

The essence of these days lies in one word: judgment. These are the days when God's court is in session, so to speak, and He judges the deeds and lives of all people. Sounds great, doesn't it? What could possibly be more appealing than judgment? Having your boss scrutinize and judge your performance at work, having a professor go over a paper with a fine-tooth comb before passing judgment in the form of a grade, or having to appear before a judge in traffic court—what could possibly be more wonderful than the bright lights of judgment? Okay, so subjection to judgment doesn't sound so appealing, but if that's the case, then what's all the fuss over Rosh Hashanah and Yom Kippur?

The answer, in a word, is caring.

That God judges us is the surest sign that there exists a meaningful and deeply caring relationship between the Designer and Creator of the universe and each and every one of us.

The existence of these days of judgment says that life is meaningful. Who we are, what we do and achieve, the efforts that we make—all of this—matters to God Himself. While Jews have always approached the High Holidays with a sense of awe, these holidays are also a celebration of our relationship with God, in light of the awareness that He cares deeply about how things are going.

Judgment may be uncomfortable but it is also a sign of love. If you want to destroy a child, don't beat her, ignore her. To a child the most devastating response to how she acts is no response at all. The most destructive message parents can possibly send their child is, I'm not interested. Children, despite what they may say, far prefer judgment to disinterest. Whether they can articulate it or not, every child knows that disinterest is the antithesis of relationship.

The message that Rosh Hashanah and Yom Kippur send is clear: to be engaged in life is to be engaged in the ultimate relationship; our choices and their consequences are of paramount importance, and God cares so deeply that He can't not judge us.

Wouldn't One Day of Awe Be Enough?

The truth is, Rosh Hashanah and Yom Kippur are *not* just one long day of judgment. It's Rosh Hashanah that is *the* day of judgment, while Yom Kippur is the day on which we confront, in the chambers of God the judge, all the things we've done wrong, and we ask for forgiveness. But there's a problem.

Why should we ask for forgiveness for our wrongdoings *after* the judgment has already taken place? Wouldn't it make more sense to first go to the judge and say, "Look, I know I've made mistakes in the past, but I regret them; they were wrong, and from now on I'm going to be a different person. What else can I say? Go ahead, judge me." In other words, shouldn't Yom Kippur come first, and then, after having pleaded our case, we can throw ourselves on the mercy of the court and brace ourselves for judgment.

From God's perspective, the Days of Awe are about caring and concern. From our perspective, they are about the nature of our commitment to the source of that caring and love. Think of it like this: Imagine that you set out to drive from Chicago to New York and instead of going east, you go west. Until you realize that you are traveling in the wrong direction, almost everything you do will be a mistake and will only take you farther and farther away from your intended destination.

Rosh Hashanah is when we stand back and reassess the direction of our lives. We ask ourselves, do we know where we want to be going, and are we headed in the right direction? Once we have a clear destination and direction in mind, only then can we look back at every turn and intersection of life and assess if they have moved us closer to where we want to go or not. That examination of the specifics of the trip is Yom Kippur—a review of the details in light of the overall goal and direction.

In terms of our relationship with God, Rosh Hashanah is a basic evaluation of our commitment to the relationship. We ask ourselves: Am I committed? How deeply am I committed? And is this relationship—this marriage—the central defining element of my life? Only after the setting straight of one's course on Rosh Hashanah does Yom Kippur become meaningful. Yom Kippur is an examination of the details of life. It's when we ask: Are the choices that I'm making—the starts and stops of life—deepening the relationship I'm so committed to or undermining it?

On Rosh Hashanah we assess, and God examines, our underlying commitment to the relationship. On Yom Kippur we assess, and God weighs, the deeds of our lives on the scales of the relationship.

So Rosh Hashanah and Yom Kippur—like Passover, Shavuot, Sukkot, and Shemini Atzeret (when you get down to their essence) are all about a relationship with God. And that is awesome indeed.

Stage III. Chanukah, Purim, the Three Weeks, and the Ninth of Av

A Golden Calf and a Rocky Marriage

You'll recall that all the holidays found in the Torah have a conceptual counterpart in the relationship between God and the Jewish people. Unfortunately, the road this marriage has taken hasn't always been the smoothest one. As a matter of fact, there have been some major potholes along the way. Two of these potholes, the building of a golden calf just days after accepting the Torah, and the destruction of the Temple in Jerusalem, were so traumatic that they altered the course of Jewish history, left palpable impressions on time itself, and created a new context for the marital relationship of God and the Jewish people. They also became the source of a new set of holidays.

Think of it like this. The relationship that blossomed at the Exodus (Passover) and matured at Mount Sinai (Shavuot) took a sudden and tragic turn for the worse just forty days after the events at Sinai. And this tragic development, though it was able to be patched up, left a scar on the relationship.

When a Lover Strays

One of the Bible's most famous stories is that of the golden calf. Picture the scene: God has just revealed Himself to the Jewish nation at Sinai; the Jewish people's commitment to accept the Torah is like a bride's commitment to be married; Moses ascends the mountain to receive the tablets from God; and then, while Moses is up on the mountain, the Jews decide to build and worship a golden calf.

So Much for that Relationship

"A shamelessly unfaithful bride: This is referring to the Jewish nation when they made the golden calf. At that instant they were like a bride at her most intimate moment who had a liaison with another. Yet, though she had to be banished, His love for her was not diminished."

Talmud, Gittin 32b, with Rashi

The famous story of the golden calf is the story of a young bride who has sneaked away for an illicit encounter. And you can just imagine how her husband felt when he realized what had happened. God's feelings, so to speak, are symbolized by the tablets that lay smashed at the foot of Mount Sinai. God is outraged and justifiably so. At the same time, our tradition tells us that despite His "outrage," and despite the fact that He threw her out of the house, He still loved her. Even more, He longed for reconciliation.

The infamous date of the golden calf and the shattered tablets was the seventeenth day of the Hebrew month of Tamuz. As it would turn out, the Seventeenth of Tamuz would become the first day of a period later commemorated as the Three Weeks. The horrible breach in the marriage that began with the golden calf on the Seventeenth of Tamuz culminated in other calamitous events that concluded on the calendar three weeks later.

A Band of Spies, a Charred Temple, but No Divorce

After smashing the tablets, Moses proceeded to have the golden calf pulverized into a heap of dust. He then spent forty days trying to patch up the relationship with God, followed by a second forty-day stint at the top of Mount Sinai. This second forty-day visit with God ended on Yom Kippur when Moses descended from the mountain with a second set of tablets and, thankfully, met with no surprises. For the next number of months, the Jews were involved in one of history's great construction projects—the building of the Tabernacle. The Tabernacle was the magnificent Temple in Jerusalem in its prefabricated, portable form. It was where the connection between God and the Jewish nation was most palpable. Shortly after construction was complete, God said that the time had come to head straight for Israel and set up shop. Unfortunately, things didn't go so smoothly.

Spies were dispatched to scout out the land, their report was bleak, the reaction of the people was even worse, and before you knew it, once again the young bride had spurned her lover. You see, the land of Israel was much more than just a homeland. It was where the Jewish people and God were destined to live together. Israel was where their relationship was meant to take root and blossom. And the heart of Israel was to be the Temple in Jerusalem, the place of deepest intimacy.

> *"When King Solomon wrote in Song of Songs '...on his wedding day and on the day of his heart's rejoicing,' The phrase 'his wedding day' is a reference to the day on which the Torah was given, and the phrase, 'the day of his heart's rejoicing' is a reference to the Temple in Jerusalem."*
>
> Talmud

The Temple in Jerusalem represents the fulfillment of the marriage between God and the Jewish people. A couple's first date, the day of their engagement, and even the wedding day itself are all one-time events. What follows these life-changing events is nothing less than a new life, a life that is an ongoing process of ever-deepening relationship, connectedness, and intimacy. This ongoing and ultimate intimacy is what the land of Israel, and at its center the Temple in Jerusalem, is all about.

When the Jewish nation in the desert said no to entering the land of Israel, what they were actually saying no to was the fulfillment of their relationship with God.

The date on which the Jews said, "The heck with it, we'd just as soon camp out right here in the desert rather than go live in Israel," was the ninth day of the Hebrew month of Av. Take a quick look at Jewish history and you will find that it is that very same day, the Ninth of Av, on which both the first and second Temples were destroyed. Take another look and you will find that the Ninth of Av arrives on the calendar exactly three weeks after the Seventeenth of Tamuz.

> *"On the Seventeenth of Tamuz the walls of the Temple were breached... and on the Ninth of Av the Temple was destroyed."*

Code of Jewish Living

When the first Temple was destroyed and the Jews were deported to Babylonia, that was exile. Then again, when the second Temple was destroyed and Jews by the hundreds of thousands were massacred and sold as slaves, this too was exile. And both of these exiles were echoes of an earlier, more seminal exile, an exile that was set in motion with the golden calf and reached its bitter crescendo with the refusal of the Jews to settle the land of Israel.

God's reaction to the Jewish people's rejection of Israel and of Him was threefold. First He said (the following is not a literal translation), "Fine, if you don't want to join me in Israel, then have it your way." As a result, that generation of Jews would spend the next thirty-eight years wandering and dying out in the Sinai desert. Second, though their relationship was never severed, those thirty-eight years of wandering were a time when the relationship took place at arm's length. In the words of Rashi, the classic medieval commentator, "From the time of the spies until the time when a new generation *was* ready to settle the land of Israel, the relationship of God and the Jewish people was devoid of tenderness and warmth." And last, God said that the ramifications of their choices were so extensive that they necessitated a whole new context for bringing their relationship to its ultimate fulfillment. Deep down the love and the commitment were still there, but the wounds were deep, and the time they would take to heal would be long. This new context for the relationship is what is known as exile, and though exile would be long, it would also be healing. The fulfillment of exile is what is known as redemption.

For the Jewish people, exile is the historical context of a relationship that must now take place across a great divide. Exile is a place of distance, of a light gone dim, and of darkness. Redemption, the end of exile, is a closing of the gap that divides, a parting of the dark and ominous clouds. It's a fresh new era of reclaimed innocence and intimacy.

Interlude: Exile and Redemption

We Can Still Make This Work

Some marriages unravel and spiral so helplessly out of control that they can never be put back together. The hurt, and eventually the hatred, is so deep that the only remedy is an end to the relationship. With other couples, though the pain and the distance are immense, they still recall the love they once shared and long to somehow, some way, restore that love. The relationship between God and the Jewish people is like that second, painfully hobbled relationship. The context in which that hobbled relationship takes place is known as exile, and Chanukah, Purim, and the Three Weeks—the holidays of exile—are the strategies for slowly rebuilding the relationship. Let's take a look.

Exile: Revealing a Lost Love

The Hebrew word for "exile," *galut*, as well as the Hebrew word for "redemption," *geula*, are both grammatically built on the same base. At first, this might seem a bit strange, since exile and redemption are about as different as night and day. However, a look at the source of those two words is quite telling. It turns out that both the word *galut* "exile," and *geula* "redemption" are derived from the Hebrew word meaning "reveal." Conceptually, what this indicates is that, while on the surface exile and redemption may seem to be vastly different states of being, beneath the surface they both serve the same purpose. Both exile and redemption are vehicles for *revealing* that which has become hidden.

Exile is the experiential realization of how much has been lost, how frightfully tenuous the connection has become. It is just this realization, the realization that we stand at the brink of losing all we love, that unleashes a new determination to recapture what we once had.

In the context of Jewish life, this means that the holidays of exile are essential for bringing to light lost dimensions of love.

Stage IV. The Holidays of Exile

There's Something Revealing Going On

Chanukah

The essence of the Chanukah story goes like this: Long, long ago the Jews were in exile and lived under the dark shadow and heavy hand of the powerful Greco-Syrian empire. The Greeks wanted the Jews to abandon their commitment to Judaism in favor of the more beautiful, refined, and universalistic culture of Greece. The Jews (though many clearly wavered) resolved never to loosen their grip on Judaism. The outgrowth of this struggle was a war, a miracle, and a holiday. The result of the war was the reclamation of the Temple in Jerusalem, the miracle was that where darkness should have reigned, eight lights burned in the Temple's Menorah, and the holiday is Chanukah.

On the surface, when we think about the lights of Chanukah, we think about the Menorah; however, on a deeper plane, we understand that it was the flame of Jewish commitment—against all odds—that truly rekindled the flames of the Menorah.

On Chanukah, though the mightiest forces on Earth tried to pry us away from God, we resolved to commit everything we had in the battle to remain committed to God. The depth of commitment achieved by the Jews at the time of Chanukah went to the heart of creation itself. On Chanukah, despite the darkness of exile, new lights were revealed.

"Chanukah alludes to the original dedication of creation, and both took place on the twenty-fifth of the month."

Rabbi Horowitz, 17th century chief rabbi of Jerusalem

"The tabernacle in the desert was completed on the 25th of Kislev. Later, at the time of the Chanukah, the Temple was rededicated on the 25th of Kislev, and the presence of God in the world, as intended since creation, was realized."

Rabbi Gedalya Schorr, 20th century scholar

Purim

The essence of the Purim story goes like this: Long, long ago the Jews lived in exile under the dominion of the mighty Persian Empire. An evil Jew-hater named Haman attained a position of political influence and prevailed on the king to murder all the Jews. In the end (to make a long story short) the king's wife Esther, herself a secret Jew, prevailed upon the king to allow the Jews to defend themselves. As a result, Haman and his cohorts were defeated, the Jews escaped with their lives, and Purim became a holiday. The details can be found in the Book of Esther.

The story of Purim is another story of exile, another story of revealing the hidden. In fact, the Hebrew words, *Megillat Esther* (the Book of Esther), literally translate as "revelation of the hidden." Of all the twenty-four books that make up the Bible, the Book of Esther is the only one in which the name of God never appears. In all other Biblical writings, God's name is spelled out and His involvement in events is clearly manifest. The Book of Esther is unique in that it only alludes to God while never mentioning Him by name. In other words, the story of Purim is the story of God being hidden from the Jewish people, yet revealing His presence.

"Though the Jews accepted the Torah at Mount Sinai, they once again reaffirmed their acceptance [after having been spared in the days of Esther]."

Talmud, Shabbat 88a

According to tradition, Jewish commitment to the Torah had become lax prior to the events of Purim and was strengthened in the wake of their salvation. At the same time, while God seemed to be utterly hidden prior to the events of Purim, His presence was subtly revealed between the lines of the unfolding salvation. This is the hide-and-seek dialectic of exile. Just as God seems to recede into the murky background of history, almost despite themselves, the Jews are able to intuit His presence. At the time of Purim, they sensed that despite the darkness of exile, God was still there, watching out and reaching out. And they reached back in the only way they knew how—by reaffirming their commitment to the Torah and to God.

The Long Way Home

The Three Weeks begin with a day of fasting on the Seventeenth of Tamuz and conclude with a day of fasting and bitter mourning on the Ninth of Av. The taste of exile is never as bitter as it is during this time period. Yet paradoxically, the Ninth of Av, the bitterest day of the year, is referred to as a *moed*, a rendezvous. But how can this be? How can a day rooted in a relationship gone sour, a day of distance and destruction, of tears and exile, possibly share the title *moed* with festivals like Passover, and Shavuot, and Sukkot?

The Ninth of Av, a day shrouded by exile, is the first step along the long road home—the road to redemption. The very moment we feel so distraught is the moment we begin to rebuild our relationship with God, and that is a *moed*, a rendezvous of love. After all, why would we be so deeply saddened, so distraught, if we didn't want so desperately for the relationship to be different?

> *"Anyone who mourns for the destruction of Jerusalem merits a glimpse of the joy that will accompany her rebuilding."*

> Talmud

The Three Weeks that culminate on the Ninth of Av are a time for coming to grips with how tenuous our relationship has become, how paltry is any perceived gain in walking out on God, and how dearly we long to restore a tarnished love. Chanukah and Purim build on these realizations.

Chanukah: With all the alluring beauty that was Athens and with the stunning culture that had attracted the devotion of so many nations, the Greeks vied for the loyalty of the Jews—and they lost. When push came to shove, as they say, the commitment of the Jewish people was to God and God alone. Even within exile, within the altered context of the relationship between God and the Jewish people, the Jews showed where their deepest commitments lie. And within exile, this was a critical step towards reconciliation.

Purim: Another reaffirmation of commitment within the context of the altered relationship. A fresh commitment to the Torah itself, to living the commitment, and to expressing the relationship in the detail of everyday life.

When taken together, the Three Weeks, Chanukah, and Purim are all about the process of rebuilding a relationship that the Jewish people had strayed from. As such, the postbiblical holidays, as much as those set forth in the Torah itself, are all days of *moed*, rendezvous days with God.

Stage Five: The Final Framework

Understanding the holidays within the framework of the ultimate relationship between God and the Jewish people—between God and every one of us—is essential to accessing life's deepest potential and meaning. In truth, we have just scratched the surface of a greater meaning of the holidays. To more fully grasp and achieve the promise of the holidays, you will have to read on far beyond the covers of this little book. I promise you will be glad you did.

> *Some marriages are meant to last forever.*
> *The marriage between God and the Jewish people*
> *is one of them.*
> *The holidays are keys to the heart—of an eternal*
> *and transcendent relationship.*

The chart on the following page is an expansion of the chart on page 10. This chart incorporates a spiritual, conceptual dimension into the historical-holiday framework.

Holiday Continuum: Marriage, History and Holidays

Commitment and engagement	Marriage; specifics of relationship	Separation	Distance	Commitment	Examining the details	Intimacy	Renewal of commitment in exile	Renewed embrace of Torah
Exodus from Egypt	Torah given at Sinai	Golden Calf; shattered tablets — Jerusalem besieged	Spies. Jews in desert refuse to enter Israel. — Temples I & II are destroyed	Creation. Adam and Eve	God forgives Jews for the Golden Calf, and gives second set of tablets	Divine Clouds protect the Jews in the desert	Revolt against Greece / Flask of oil burns for eight days	Esther and Mordecai save the Jews from Haman
Passover	Shavuot	Seventeenth of Tamuz	Ninth of Av	Rosh Hashanah	Yom Kippur	Sukkot / Shemini Atzeret	Chanukah	Purim
15-21 Nisan	6 Sivan	17 Tamuz	9 Av	1-2 Tishrei	10 Tishrei	15-21 Tishrei / 22 Tishrei	25 Kislev-3 Tevet	14 & 15 Adar
March/April	May/June	June/July	July	September	October	October	December	April

the nuts and bolts of the
Holidays

3

A Hands-on Guide to Celebrating the Holidays

So You Say You Want to Celebrate

Let's paaaarrtyyy!!!

Oops, I mean happy Chanukah, or happy Passover, or good *yom tov, shana tova, chag sameach*, have an easy fast—anyway, you get the picture.

This section is designed to serve as a starting point for your experience of the holidays. An exhaustive treatment of each holiday would require an entire book, or at least a chapter, about each holiday. My hope is that this all too brief section will provide you with a basic framework for participating in the wondrous events that fill the Jewish calendar—and Jewish life—and a basis from which to build further understanding. Common aspects shared by all holidays such as the family holiday meals, attending synagogue, prayers, and Torah readings will not be addressed here. Rather, we will highlight many of the distinguishing elements central to each holiday. Each will be addressed separately, and in the context of each we will highlight five areas:

1. **Star of the Show**—The central practices and command-ments (*mizvot*) of the holiday.
2. **Supporting Cast**—This will highlight various customs related to the holiday.
3. **Technical Stuff**—Here we will discuss props, like the menorah and the seder plate, practical aspects of observance, and relevant blessings.
4. **Kidz Zone**—A few suggestions for making the holiday particularly relevant for children and families.
5. **Tidbits for the Soul**—Brief insights into the meaning behind the practices, customs, and props.

Let's begin with Rosh Hashanah, the Jewish New Year.

Rosh Hashanah

Star of the Show

The Shofar: The sounding of the shofar in synagogue is the central feature of Rosh Hashanah. The Biblical commandment is "to hear" the sound of the shofar. In Judaism, to hear means "to understand." The call of the shofar is a sound whose purpose is to inspire us to reflect upon and more deeply understand the issues that are most important to us in life.

The blowing of the shofar consists of three different notes—*tekiah*, *teruah*, and *shevarim*—and each is intended to evoke a particular idea and feeling. The *tekiah* calls us from routine day-to-day living, from a dissipation of our creative energies to refocus on who it is we truly want to be. The *teruah* is more comforting and allows us to integrate the thoughts and feelings of the day. The *shevarim* is an anxious, longing note. It evokes the yearning to somehow start again, this time accomplishing what we want in life.

Supporting Cast

Apple in Honey: On the night of Rosh Hashanah, people gather for a festive dinner that includes dipping a piece of apple in honey. This represents our heartfelt wishes for a sweet year for ourselves, our families, and for the Jewish people. There is also a custom to eat other foods that symbolize our thoughts and hopes at the beginning of the new year. These include pomegranates, whose many seeds represent our wishes for a year chock-full of kind and meritorious deeds; dates (the Hebrew word for date means "destroy"), representing our hope that our enemies disappear; and others.

Tashlich: This is the custom of reciting certain prayers by a river or other body of water. When traveling, rivers can be obstacles along the way. From the time of Abraham until today, Jews have always faced obstacles on the journey of life. As the new year begins, we express our commitment to our life goals, despite the obstacles and challenges that will surely come our way. There is also a custom to empty one's pockets into the river and symbolically watch our past misdeeds float away.

Technical Stuff

The minimum number of shofar blasts one is required to hear is nine—three sets of each of the three notes; however, the accepted manner of blowing actually results in many more sounds. Different synagogues have different customs about when the shofar is sounded during the service, but as a rule, in total, one hundred blasts are sounded.

Kidz Zone

A more beautiful family: The Hebrew word *shofar* means to "polish or beautify." On Rosh Hashanah we think about how to polish our character and become more beautiful human beings. Every family has its issues. This is a wonderful time for families to talk about what can be done to enhance the beauty of their relationships. Together, parents and children can commit to doing one thing in the coming year to make the family's life an even more beautiful experience.

Rosh Hashanah cards: Children can design their own personalized cards for relatives and friends.

One-of-a-Kind honey jars: Why settle for a plastic tube of honey when there is no end to the wonderful ways in which children can decorate everything from styrofoam cups to homemade clay jars?

Tidbits for the Soul

Each and every one of us is a unique world of potential. On Rosh Hashanah we pray for life—for a life brimming with the realization of our potential.

Yom Kippur

Star of the Show

The Fast: The fast of Yom Kippur begins just prior to nightfall on the eve of the holiday and continues until sunset the next day. The purpose of fasting is to temporarily put our physical needs on hold in order to focus on our souls.

Teshuva: We all want to do what's right in life, but sometimes we rationalize and do what we feel like doing instead. Sound familiar? One of the most common words in the Yom Kippur prayer book is "sin." In Hebrew, the generic term for sin is *chet*, which literally means "to make a mistake." The issue on Yom Kippur is this: How do we correct the mistakes of our past and avoid repeating them in the future? This is *teshuva*. The common translation of *teshuva* is "repentance." The proper translation of the word *teshuva* is "to return." *Teshuva* is an animated technique for locating the rationalizations that lie at the root of our mistakes, recognizing them, dealing with them, and eliminating them. The *teshuva* process has four parts: feeling regret and a sense of loss about one's mistakes, the identification and abandonment of rationalizations, a commitment to not repeating the same mistakes, and a verbal admission to God and anyone who suffered from your mistakes.

Supporting Cast

Kol Nidre: The *Kol Nidre* service on the night of Yom Kippur is probably the most well-attended of all services. *Kol Nidre* is about the awesome power of words and about the credibility of our verbal commitments. In essence, at *Kol Nidre* we reflect on the following question, "When I give my word to people or to God, can I be counted on to live up to what I have said?"

Blessing one's children: There is a little-known but beautiful blessing that parents give to their children on Yom Kippur eve; it's printed in many prayer books. This blessing is a powerful and inspiring way to begin the holiday.

Technical Stuff

In addition to not eating or drinking, there are four other prohibitions that move our focus away from our physical needs. They are: not washing or bathing for comfort or pleasure; not using body lotions, creams, and the like; not wearing leather shoes; and not engaging in marital relations.

Kidz Zone

Sorry: Children can be encouraged to make an "I'm sorry, I did it, I won't do it again" list, and to apologize to family and friends before Yom Kippur. If a personal apology is too uncomfortable, they can write a note. Parents should let their children know that they too are making the same sort of list. It's quite healthy for kids to see that adults can admit to mistakes, and are also trying to do better.

I'm hungry: The length of time that children fast depends on age and ability. For young children, it may be enough just to not have any candy or special treats for the day; for others, a partial fast is appropriate. By the age of *bar* or *bat mitzva*, they should be ready to go the distance.

Tidbits for the Soul

Yom Kippur is a day for speaking to God. In prayer we address God as "You;" it's direct and personal. Yom Kippur affords plenty of time to speak to God honestly, openly, and from the heart. This is the key to everything.

Sukkot

Star of the Show

The Sukkah: A *sukkah* is a temporary residence that Jews construct and live in during the week-long holiday of Sukkot. Typically, a family will build a small (usually around 10 feet by 10 feet, though it's common to find much larger *sukkahs*) wooden shed that has no roof. The roof, however, is considered the most important element of the *sukkah*. While the *sukkah* itself is a temporary, makeshift structure, the roof is even more impermanent. The roof must be made out of plant cuttings as opposed to conventional building materials, and it also can't be solid; this means that one has to be able to see the sky through gaps in the roof.

Four Species: Four plant species are bundled together and "waved" during the holiday. The four species, known collectively as the "*esrog* and *lulav*," are the fruit of the beautiful *esrog* (citron) tree and branches from the date palm, brook willow, and myrtle. If you've never seen a four species bundle, I suggest you visit a Jewish bookstore a week or two before Sukkot.

Supporting Cast

Think of it as a villa: As much as possible, we are supposed to transfer our home's primary activities into the *sukkah*. This includes eating, reading, relaxing, and sleeping. For all intents and purposes—and weather permitting—the *sukkah* replaces our home, apartment, or condo for the entire week of the holiday.

Technical Stuff

How to wave your esrog and lulav: Explaining how to wave a *lulav* to someone who has never seen it done is kind of like teaching someone who has never seen a bicycle how to ride one. Here goes.

1. Hold the *lulav* in your right hand and the *esrog* in your left hand. 2. Recite the blessing below. 3. After saying the blessing, bring your hands together so that all four species form one group. 4. Shake your bundle three times in all six directions: forward, to the right, behind you, to the left, up, and then downward.

Blessing:

*Baruch atah Adonai Eloheinu melech ha'olam
asher kidishanu b'mitzvotav v'tzivanu al n'tilat lulav.*

Blessed are You, *Adonai* our God, King of the Universe, Who has made us holy through His commandments and has commanded us concerning taking the lulav.

Kidz Zone

Esrog box: As a rule, *esrogs* come in small, white cardboard boxes. There is no end to how these can be decorated—puffy paints, glitter, marker, etc.—or children can make their own custom designed boxes.

Esrog and lulav: Younger children can use colored construction paper to make their own *esrog* and *lulav*.

Decorations: Traditionally, children are very involved in making all sorts of decorations for the family *sukkah*. Decorations can be saved from year to year, and serve as a fun measure of how children's creative talents blossom over the years.

Tidbits for the Soul

The four species correspond to four parts of the body. The palm branch (*lulav*) corresponds to the spine, the citron (*esrog*) is the heart, the myrtle leaves (*hadassim*) are the eyes, and the leaves of the willow (*aravot*) are the lips. On Sukkot, we hold and wave each of the four species—each of the four different parts of ourselves—together in one bundle. The four species represent inner-harmony, and the six directions represent every dimension of life. The four species have the ability to help us move toward a harmony that arises when we are able to synthesize the disparate aspects of our being in every realm of life.

Shemini Atzeret

Star of the Show

Synagogue: Shemini Atzeret is a dual-identity holiday. The first day is only Shemini Atzeret, and the second day is both Shemini Atzeret and Simchat Torah. In addition to a holiday meal, the focus of the first day is the prayers, and Torah reading in synagogue.

Dancing: The second day of Shemini Atzeret is the conclusion of the High Holiday season. While the Torah doesn't require anything unique on Shemini Atzeret, the Jewish people themselves instituted what came natural to them—they embraced the Torah and danced all night and all day—it's called Simchat Torah, and it's a truly marvelous culmination to the holidays.

Supporting Cast

Being called to the Torah: The honor of being called upon to recite a blessing before the reading of the Torah in synagogue is called an *aliyah*. Unlike Shabbat and the holidays, on Simchat Torah *everyone* gets an aliyah. Additionally, Simchat Torah is the only time when children also receive an aliyah. There is an ancient and beautiful custom to call all the children at once to the Torah and to spread a large *tallit* (prayer shawl) over their heads.

Kidz Zone

Flags: Younger children often dance in synagogue with flags and homemade Torahs. These flags and Torahs make for great pre-holiday family art projects.

Let's dance: The experiences of youth can set the tone for so much of what follows in life. A child's experience of dancing with her parents in synagogue can make all the difference in the world about how that child will relate to her Jewish identity. A child who dances in synagogue learns that it's a joy to be a Jew.

Tidbits for the Soul

The Hebrew words *shemini atzeret* mean, "the lingering eighth." Instead of an abrupt departure from the holidays, we linger for just one more day. The ability to linger—to hold on for just a while longer—is a key to integrating spiritual experiences into our lives.

Chanukah

Star of the Show

The Menorah: The menorah is an eight-branched candelabra. The eight flames of the menorah represent the miraculous eight days that the original menorah stayed lit when the Jews liberated the Temple in Jerusalem. On the first night of Chanukah one candle is lit, and on each of the following nights, an additional candle is lit until the final night when all eight flames are illuminated.

The lights of the menorah challenge us to keep the flame of Judaism burning in an often dark and hostile world.

Supporting Cast

Latkes: Unlike other holidays, there is no requirement to have a special meal on Chanukah. There are, however, special foods that add to the festive atmosphere of Chanukah. The miracle of Chanukah centered around the oil that burned for eight days. For this reason it is customary to prepare foods that are fried in oil; hence, the potato pancake, known as the *latke*. In Israel today, the *latke* has run into some stiff competition. *Sufganiyot*, fried jelly-filled donuts, have captured a large segment of the Chanukah market.

Technical Stuff

Left to Right: The procedure for lighting the menorah can be confusing; it works like this. On the first night you light one candle that has been placed on the far right-hand side of the menorah. That's easy enough; now here's the tricky part. After the first night you add new candles for the subsequent nights from right to left; however, you light them moving from left to right. Let's take night three as an example.

Night three: Candle number one is placed in the holder to your far right, candle number two is placed in the holder immediately to the left of candle number one, and candle number three is placed immediately to the left of candle number two. Now that you've lined them up properly, it's time to switch directions for the actual lighting. The first candle you light is the one to your far left, and then, moving to your right, you light the other candles, always ending with the one to your extreme right.

The following blessing is recited before lighting the menorah:

Baruch atah Adonai Eloheinu melech ha'olam asher kidishanu b'mitzvotav v'tzivanu lhadlik ner shel chanukah.

Blessed are You, *Adonai* our God, King of the Universe,
Who has made us holy through His commandments
and has commanded us to kindle the light of Chanukah.

*Baruch atah Adonai Eloheinu melech ha'olam
she'asah nisim la'avoteinu bayamim ha'heim bazman hazeh.*
Blessed are You, Adonai our God, King of the Universe, Who did miracles for our forefathers, in those days at this very time.

*Baruch atah Adonai Eloheinu melech ha'olam
she'hechiyanu v'kiyimanu v'higiyanu lazman hazeh.*
Blessed are You, Adonai our God, King of the Universe, Who has kept us alive, sustained us and enabled us to arrive at this season.

Kidz Zone

Dreidel: In the time of the Greeks, the study of the Torah was forbidden; nonetheless, Jews took the ultimate risk to preserve their heritage. They would secretly study Torah, and when they heard the Greek soldiers approaching, they quickly took out dreidels and began to play. The centuries-old custom of playing dreidel recalls the great risk Jews made to preserve their heritage. Dreidels can be purchased with instructions on how to play. A good game of dreidel and a plate of homemade latkes make for a wonderful evening for the whole family.

Tidbits for the Soul

The flames of the menorah are small and silent. On the first night of Chanukah we light one candle—one flame—small and silent. We walk into the room, and we barely notice its presence. It's there, but it's very subtle. Like the subtle presence of the flame, there burns within each of us a glowing yet subtle presence—our souls.

Purim

Star of the Show

The Megillah: The Book of Esther, known as *Megillat Esther*, is read in synagogue twice on Purim, once at night and again during the day. There is an obligation to hear the *megillah* read twice. If you don't understand Hebrew, that's okay; you can follow along using an English translation. It's helpful to read the *megillah* once before Purim to familiarize yourself with the flow of the story.

Mishloach manot: There is a wonderful obligation to send a gift of food, known as *shaloch manot*, to at least one person on Purim. Each gift must contain a minimum of two types of food, needs to arrive during the day of Purim, and should ideally be delivered by a third party.

Matanos l'evyonim: Another beautiful *mitzva* (spiritual directive) is to give gifts of money to at least two poor people on Purim. If you don't know any poor people, try contacting a synagogue because many establish special funds that are delivered to the poor on Purim. The sending of food gifts and gifts to the poor is meant to spur feelings of camaraderie and unity among Jews.

Purim meal: A particularly festive meal is a required part of the Purim celebration. The wearing of costumes and an extra sip or two of wine go a long way towards creating the right atmosphere.

Supporting Cast

Costumes: In the story of Purim, God seemed to be hidden in history, and the name of God never appears in the Book of Esther.

The theme of concealment runs throughout the story of Purim and. is incorporated into the holiday through the wearing of costumes.

Gragger: The arch-enemy of the Jews was Haman. There is a custom to make noise every time Haman's name is read in the *megillah*, and the traditional noise maker is called a *gragger*. This custom makes for a highly unusual and uniquely joyous atmosphere during the reading of the *megillah*.

Kidz Zone

Family megillah: An illustrated family *megillah* is a great project that people of all ages can participate in. It works like this: a) As a family, read the Book of Esther and take note of one or two central scenes in each of the ten chapters. b) Each family member is assigned different scenes to draw or illustrate as they choose. c) Take everyone's papers, tape them together, and then roll them around a can. Presto, a customized family megillah.

Shaloch manot baskets: Another great family project is decorating baskets or other containers that will be used for sending the gifts of food.

Tidbits for the Soul

Stripped of our usual attire and no longer able to rely on the externalities of clothing to define us, we are free to explore a very personal inner-world. Masquerading has a paradoxical way of allowing us to see who we really are. When I put on a face that is not—and never could be—mine, I am able to look within and ask myself, "Who, then, am I?"

Passover

Star of the Show

Matzah: Perhaps the most ubiquitous of all holiday observances, matzah is the defining element of this week-long festival. Matzah is bread with an identity crisis. On the one hand, it is "the bread of affliction" that the Jews ate when they were slaves in Egypt. At the same time, matzah is the unleavened bread representing freedom which the Jews took with them when they were liberated.

The Seder: The seder is a combination family reunion, holiday dinner, and theatrical spectacle where we recount the story of bondage and liberation.The seder addresses people's need to know where they come from. A Jewish child who grows up without the annual experience of a seder is at risk of becoming a person without a history—a person in search of place and purpose. The seder is where parents give children a sense of rootedness and belonging, of identity and direction.

Supporting Cast

The Haggadah: The *haggadah* is the text that defines and directs the seder. It is a combination history book, Magna Carta, mission statement, and road map for the seder. Next to the Torah itself, the *haggadah* is one of the most important of all Jewish texts.

Technical Stuff

In addition to the reading of the *haggadah*, the seder also features drinking four cups of wine, eating bitter herbs, dipping a vegetable in salt water, eating matzah, asking the four questions, searching for the *afikomen*, and other observances and customs designed to bring the experience of slavery and redemption to life.

Kidz Zone

1. Matzah bakery: Some cities have bakeries that are only used once a year for the baking of handmade matzah. If there is one in your city, take your children to see matzah being baked. In cities where there isn't such a bakery, some synagogues send a delegation of members to help bake matzah for their community. Find out if there is such a group in your city, and join them.

2. Seder props: All sorts of craft projects can be made for use at the seder. Large white paper plates can be painted and become beautiful seder plates; styrofoam cups can be transformed into the Cup of Elijah, and there is no end to homemade plagues like frogs and wild animals. The seder, with all of its rich symbolism, is a particularly appropriate time to encourage children to make a creative contribution the experience.

Tidbits for the Soul

On the night of Passover, the night of liberation, we are able to see where we have been stifled, and to detect a way toward freedom.

Shavuot

Star of the Show

Just a meal: No shofar, no matzah, nothing—just a festive holiday meal. Why? Because on Shavuot we received the Torah, and the essence of the Torah is to engage and elevate the physicality of life in service of spirituality. So we sit down to a meal, and we ask ourselves "Am I eating solely to entertain my taste buds, or am I eating to energize my body so that it can best pursue the agenda of my soul?"

Supporting Cast

Torah study: There is a custom to stay up all night on Shavuot and study the Torah until sunrise. If you can't make it through the whole night, an hour or two is also great.

Counting the omer: Beginning with the second night of Passover, one counts the days and weeks until Shavuot. This counting is done every night. The precise wording for the counting is printed in most prayerbooks after the evening service.

Kidz Zone

Mount Sinai: Make a model of Mount Sinai before the holiday. Depending on ages, this can range from a simple drawing to a three-D model of the mountain with the Jewish people camped at its foot.

The big ten: Memorize the Ten Commandments with your children. Be sure to give them some kind of reward for their achievement.

Go for it: Take your children to a synagogue that is hosting an all night Torah study event. Even if you are only there for an hour, children find it exciting to be a part of the action.

Tidbits for the Soul
Sometimes Jews seem to have everything in common while at other times we seem to have almost nothing in common. What is it that nourishes our sense of collective identity, of peoplehood, of being a part of a larger family?

> "It [the Torah] gave to the Jews, through the two thousand years of wandering which they were soon to begin, a 'portable Fatherland,' as Heine were to call it, an intangible and spiritual state; it kept them united despite every dispersion, proud despite every defeat, and brought them across the centuries to our own time, a strong and apparently indestructible people."
>
> Will Durant, *The Story of Civilization* [6]

Seventeenth of Tamuz and the Three Weeks

Star of the Show
Fasting and reflection: The Seventeenth of Tamuz, unlike Yom Kippur, is a daytime fast only. The fast begins with the break of day, and concludes at nightfall. While the fast is essential, its purpose is to spur one to reflect on the spiritual messages inherent in the day.

Supporting Cast
The Three Weeks: The Three Weeks between the Seventeenth of Tamuz and the Ninth of Av is a period of national mourning for the destruction of Jerusalem and the Temple. This is a period of time during which it is appropriate to limit joyous activities. Various restrictions related to mourning apply during the Three Weeks.

Technical Stuff
The intensity of the mourning and the related restrictions increase as the Ninth of Av draws nearer. From the Seventeenth

of Tamuz until the first of Av, weddings are not performed, and one refrains from listening to music as well as shaving or having one's hair cut. Beginning with the first of Av, prohibitions include not eating meat or drinking wine, and other restrictions.

Kidz Zone

Learn about Jerusalem: Israel and Jerusalem have always been at the center of Jewish consciousness. I want to recommend two wonderful books for children. For younger children, *Take Me to the Holy Land*, by Tsivia Yanofsky, and for older children (and adults), *Jerusalem, the Eye of the Universe: A Pictorial Tour of the Holy City*, by Aryeh Kaplan.

Maps and models: Homemade maps of Israel and models of the Temple or the Western Wall—from the very simple to the most detailed and elaborate—when placed around the home, serve to keep the message of the Three Weeks at the forefront of everyone's thoughts.

Tidbits for the Soul

> *"Jerusalem is not merely the capital of our country, but also the bedrock of our existence—the nexus of Jewish national and religious life. Over two decades ago, I said to a Soviet court about to sentence me to fifteen years in prison for my work as a Jewish activist, 'For 2,000 years the Jewish people, my people, have been dispersed all over the world, and seemingly deprived of any hope of returning. But still, each year Jews have stubbornly, and apparently without reason, said to each other,* **Leshana haba'a b'yirusholayim!** *(Next Year in Jerusalem!) And today, when I am further than ever from my dream, from my people, and from my wife Avital, and when many difficult years of prison and camps lie ahead of me, I say to my wife and my people,* **Leshana haba'a b'yirusholayim!***"*

Natan Sharansky, Israeli Parliament member [7]

The Ninth of Av, Tisha B'Av

Star of the Show

Fasting and tears: The Ninth of Av, like Yom Kippur, is a full twenty-four hour fast. The fast begins before nightfall and concludes at sunset. In addition to fasting, because it is a day when we feel an intense sense of loss, it is appropriate to cry, like a mourner who has lost a loved one, over the calamities of the Ninth of Av.

Supporting Cast

Lamentations and Elegies: As a sign of mourning, people sit on the floor during the special Ninth of Av prayer service. During this service, the biblical Book of Lamentations is recited as well as special poetic essays known as Elegies (*Kinot*). These readings focus on the tragedies of Jewish history from the earliest times through the Crusades and the Holocaust.

Technical Stuff

In addition to fasting, other prohibitions include not bathing or washing, not wearing leather shoes, not greeting people with the usual "good morning," and not sitting on a chair or couch until noon.

Kidz Zone

Synagogue: The evening service, when synagogue lights are dimmed and everyone is sitting on the floor, can make a powerful impression on children. Even if they can't stay for the entire service, it's worthwhile for them to be there even for a short while.

Recommended reading: The Artscroll Children's Holiday Series by Yaffa Ganz includes an excellent book about the Ninth of Av.

Tidbits for the Soul

The Temple was destroyed, because Jews, for no good reason, despised and spoke bitterly about one another. The Three Weeks and the Ninth of Av are times when one should go out of one's way to demonstrate a sense of caring and bonding with all Jews.

just when you thought you knew it *All*

4

A Collection of Mini-essays Exploring New
Dimensions of the Holidays

It's All in the Holidays

> *"Moses devoted more time to explaining the holidays than any other aspect of the Torah. This was because contained within the holidays are the essential concepts for understanding and living a life of personal and spiritual growth."*
>
> Commentary of the Netziv, Numbers 30:1

This section contains a selection of essays that reveal how some of Judaism's central ideas are woven into the fabric of the holidays. These ideas (and many others that are simply beyond the scope of a Nutshell book) will provide you with fresh perspectives on the holidays, Judaism, and life. Enjoy!

The Big Bang Theory of Rosh Hashanah

Judgment? Think Again

We have all lived through days of judgment—days when the past has come back to haunt us. In the Torah portion for the first day of Rosh Hashanah we find the following statement.

> *"And God heard the voice of the young boy, and then an angel of God called to Hagar from heaven and said to her, 'What is the matter with you, Hagar? Do not be afraid, for God has heard the voice of the young boy right where he is.'"*

Genesis 21:17-18

Reflecting on this verse, the sages of the Talmud offer a mystifying perspective on Rosh Hashanah. This "young boy" was Yishmael, Abraham's son. Even as a young boy, Yishmael was a cold-blooded murderer. In the future he and his descendants would become bitter oppressors of the Jewish people.

Yishmael lay there abandoned, left to die. But God caused Hagar to notice a well and she was able to draw water and save the life of Yishmael. Why? That Yishmael had an evil past was well known; that his future would sow seeds of even greater evil and destruction—this was also known to God.

But Yishmael was being judged *at that moment*, "right where he was." Our sages tell us that the dynamics of judgment as they applied to Yishmael apply to us, too. On Rosh Hashanah, God looks at us "right where we are." At first blush, our sages have given us good reason to breathe a sigh of relief. Think about it. Right where you are! God, though He knows the future, will not take it into account. Fair enough. But think about this—God won't even take our past into account. All we have to do is be on our best behavior for one day, and everything will be fine. The future doesn't count, the past is irrelevant, we will only be judged according to who we are on the day of Rosh Hashanah itself.

Sounds great, except for the fact that it isn't just and doesn't make sense.

When the sages made their comment, they were asking us to think for a moment and take a second look at the meaning of Rosh Hashanah as the day of judgment.

Explosive Potential

Current theory regarding the nature of the origin of the universe is commonly referred to as the Big Bang Theory. What preceded the big bang was an infinitesimally small mathematical point that was not made up of matter, contained no energy, occupied no space, and preceded time itself. Paradoxically, this inconceivably tiny point contained within it the entire universe.

This tiny primordial point represents ultimate potential. Whatever it was, when it "exploded," it unleashed an entire universe. From gravity to time and from protons to cockroaches, they were all present in some form at the instant the big bang took place.

Rosh Hashanah is the big bang. On Rosh Hashanah, we neither ponder our future nor grapple with our past. On Rosh Hashanah, we confront our ultimate potential.

Each one of us is destined to explode. Each one of us—with the choices we make in life—will create an entire universe. Each one of us possesses a profoundly immense and unique potential. The question is this: Will the universe we create be a true reflection of the potential we possess?

Rosh Hashanah is the day of judgment. Yet never once during the prayers on Rosh Hashanah do we mention our past or ask for any kind of forgiveness. For this we wait until Yom Kippur. But that's odd. How can we be judged if we don't deal with our past deeds?

The answer is that we all make mistakes in life, mistakes that move us further and further from a realization of our potential. If we are not wholeheartedly committed to pursuing a path toward our ultimate potential, then we are inevitably doomed to repeat the mistakes of our past and find new ways to move ever further from our potential, from being the person we truly want to be and can be.

There is a famous story about an elderly sage named Reb Zusia. Reb Zusia lay on his deathbed surrounded by his students and disciples. Reb Zusia was crying, and there was no one who could comfort him.

One student offered, "You were almost as wise as Moses himself." Another followed, saying, "You were almost as kind as our father Abraham," and so on. Yet Reb Zusia would not be comforted. He wept as the end drew near.

"When I pass from this world and appear before the heavenly tribunal," Reb Zusia said, "they won't ask me, 'Zusia, why weren't you as wise as Moses or as kind as Abraham?' Rather they will ask me, 'Why weren't you Zusia?' Why didn't I fulfill my potential? Why didn't I follow the path that could have been mine?"

On Rosh Hashanah, we confront our potential as human beings, but even more, as Jews. The question is one of commitment. The issue is one of judgment.

The Body and Soul of Yom Kippur

Body and Soul: Want Versus Feel

The image our sages use to capture the internal dynamics of human life is a horse and rider. This is their picture of the human condition.

A basic tension in life is the tension between what we want to do and what we feel like doing. Recognize the tension? It works like this: I *want* to help my son with his homework, but I feel like relaxing in front of the television. I want to cut my cholesterol intake, but I feel like having a piece of cheesecake. I want to visit my parents, but I feel like playing tennis. I want to make a difference with my life, but I feel like hanging out by the pool. I want to achieve the greatness of my potential, but I feel like settling for being average.

The rider—what we *want* to do—that's our soul. The horse—what we *feel* like doing—that's our body. Mind you, Judaism never denigrates the body or physical pleasures. Quite the opposite. Judaism asserts that the pleasures of the physical world are here to be enjoyed, to be fully partaken of. There is just one question. Who is in control? Is this a skilled rider in command of a powerful, yet obedient horse, or is this a rider who has lost control and is at the mercy of his horse's every whim and desire?

Fasting: Discovering a Deeper Hunger

James Kent, a graduate student at the University of California at Santa Cruz, wrote the GigAssembler, a massive computer program that helped assemble the human genome.

> *"He's unbelievable," Dr. David Haussler said. "The program represents an amount of work that would have taken a team of 5 or 10 programmers at least six months or a year. Jim in four weeks created the GigAssembler by working day and night. He had to ice his wrists at night because of the fury with which he created this extraordinarily complex piece of code."*
>
> New York Times, 2/13/01

> *"If you never wanted something so badly that you didn't forget about hunger and sleep, then you never wanted anything at all. Perhaps you have never lived."*
>
> Anonymous

The opportunity of Yom Kippur is to realign our living with the values, ideals, and goals we truly want to live for. In Jewish thought, the soul is understood to have five dimensions. On Yom Kippur, we are enjoined to remove ourselves from five types of physical comfort and desire. This temporary disassociation from physical needs both reminds us that there is another, deeper dimension to life and liberates us to devote this deepest part of who we are to becoming the person we truly long to be.

Sukkot: If I Can't Find an *Esrog,* Will a Lemon Do?

I Did It My Way

Do the following words sound familiar?

"Frankly, I consider myself to be a spiritual person. I don't really need all these rituals and details to feel close to God. I relate to God in a way that feels right to me, and I'm sure that's okay with Him." In other words, does it really matter all that much if I use an *esrog* or a lemon on Sukkot, if I shake a palm branch or a cornstalk, or if I sit in a *sukkah* or in a tent?

The holiday of Sukkot is brimming with all sorts of nitpicking details. The question is, do they really matter?

The Spirituality Is in the Details

The definition of spirituality is to have a relationship with God.

In any relationship of genuine closeness, three essential components must always be kept in mind:

1. We can have meaningful relationships only if we relate to people in terms of who they are, not in terms of who we would like them to be.

This means that if we try to superimpose our desires about who a person should be and then relate to this projected image, the result will be that we are barely relating at all. Instead, we will just be serving our own needs and thereby ensuring a hollow, lifeless relationship.

2. The relationships that are most important to us are those in which we pay the closest attention to detail.

The reason parents are so concerned about the details of their children's lives and behavior is because they love them so much. In almost any area of life, the more important the whole, the more precious its details become.

3. Our involvement and commitment to the relationship has to be sincere and genuine.

When you say to the bank teller, "Have a nice day," it's not that you don't mean it, because you do. It's just that in truth, once you leave that bank, you're not going to give the quality of that person's day another moment's thought. And the reason is that your relationship begins and ends at the teller's window. The cornerstone relationships of life—husband and wife, good friends, parents and children—are relationships that we carry with us wherever we go.

Spirituality Is a Relationship with God

The Jewish paradigm for spirituality is a relationship—a relationship with God, the transcendent Creator of all that exists. While the possibility for frail, small, and limited people to relate to an infinite Creator can seem overwhelming, if not impossible, Judaism asserts that not only is this relationship possible, but it is the source of all spirituality.

The achievement of an authentic and intimate relationship with God rests on three foundations. First, we can't relate to God in terms of who we want Him to be or in ways that feel right to us; rather, the relationship must be in terms of who He actually is and what He informs us is appropriate for the relationship to flourish. Second, we need to appreciate that just like every moment, every word, and every gesture in a marriage can hold within it the seeds of closeness, the same is true with God. Each moment of life is a moment rich with the possibility of creating a deeper and more intimate relationship with our Creator. And finally, we have to be sincerely committed to the relationship. Going through the motions just isn't good enough.

This is why, even to God, details matter. God isn't some micromanaging, detail-obsessed control freak. He is the source of all existence, from the vast and awesome galaxies to the tiny fingernail on a newborn baby all the way down to details like an *esrog* and not a lemon, or a *sukkah* and not a tent. When God lays out the details of a *mitzva*, a commandment, He's just telling us how we need to relate if we want to achieve ultimate closeness—ultimate spirituality.

Chanukah and the Family

Family Values

Many people will tell you that almost all the major ills in our society can be traced to a breakdown in the fabric of our families and a general loss of family values. In a not-so-subtle way, Chanukah is about family values, as well as the value of the family.

According to Jewish law, the ideal place for a menorah is not on a table or mantel but rather at the left side of the door as one enters a house. The menorah is positioned in this fashion so that the entrance to one's home will be "surrounded by *mitzvot*." The menorah will be on the left side of the door and the mezuzzah on the right side. On Chanukah, the symbols and ideas of the mezuzzah, the menorah, and the Jewish home are all mingled together.

Every mezuzzah, no matter how simple or elaborate the exterior may be, contains the exact same piece of parchment. Inscribed on this parchment is the statement of *Shema Yisrael*: "Hear O' Israel, the Lord our God, the Lord is One." This sentence, along with the two other paragraphs written on the parchment, contains the essence of Judaism. A Jewish home, more than anything else, is meant to be a place for fostering Jewish values and ideals. It's meant to be a place where not only family, friends, and neighbors will feel welcome, but so will God. The mezuzzah on our doorpost reminds us that a home is a place for learning, for growth, and for spirituality, not just a shelter from the rain.

The Families of Chanukah

In many ways, the Jewish home and the Jewish family are central to Chanukah. The revolt against the Greeks was spearheaded by a family, the Hasmoneans. Another family, Chanah and her seven sons (all of whom gave their lives rather than deny their devotion to God), stands as the ultimate symbol of dedication to Judaism. Additionally, according to Jewish law, one should always try to light the menorah when the entire family is gathered together. The Talmudic terminology for the obligation to light the menorah on Chanukah is *ner ish u'bayso*, "one candle for each man and his household."

During Chanukah, one's front door, the entranceway to Jewish family life, is to be surrounded by *mitzvot*. The mezuzzah calls our mind to the values and ideals that are taught and discussed and lived in a Jewish home, while the menorah reminds us of the willingness of the Jewish people, and particularly of Jewish families, to fight for the survival of the Jewish home and Jewish life.

The story of the Jewish people is the story of the Jewish family. We are a nation of families and a family that is a nation. For the Jewish people, Jewish survival and Jewish revival begin and end in the Jewish home.

The Unity of Purim

The Meaning of Jewish Unity

Before Esther would approach the king on behalf of the Jews, she said to Mordecai, "Go and gather together all the Jews." Esther realized that Jewish unity and Jewish survival go hand in hand.

Jewish solidarity is not optional for the Jewish people. The existence of the Jewish people is predicated on our unity, a unity that expresses itself as the full-fledged mutual responsibility of brotherhood.

Our sages teach us that, just prior to the receiving of the Torah at Mount Sinai, the Jewish people achieved a degree of unity that they characterized as "being like one person with one heart." It is no coincidence that the Jewish people achieved this state of indivisibility at the foot of Mount Sinai. A profound sense of national harmony was considered to be an essential prerequisite to the giving of the Torah.

Giving, the Gift of Unity

One of the central elements of Purim is the *mishloach manot*, the sending of gifts of food to other people.

To the contemporary lament of Jewish disunity, Purim offers the following response and suggestion: send gifts. The way to access our latent capacity for expressing the existential reality of Jewish oneness is by expressing benevolence to one another.

Rabbi Eliyahu E. Dessler, a major twentieth century expositor of Jewish thought, taught that when people choose to give of themselves to another—whether they are giving a gift of food, time, money, or expertise—the very act of giving draws them closer. When I give of myself to another, I am, in essence, transferring a part of myself to the recipient. I am planting a bit of my being into the soil of someone else's life. And as we implant bits of ourselves into one another, we are naturally drawn together. We begin to see and care for one another in a new light. As we are aware of ourselves—sensitive and responsive to our own needs—so we become sensitized to the needs of others in whom a portion of ourselves now exists.

On Purim, we do more than just give gifts; in fact, rather than hand them to one another, we are supposed to *send* them with someone who delivers them on our behalf. The question is why? Why is it essential that our food baskets be delivered by someone else? This practice is meant to highlight the idea that each of us must be ready to serve as a force for facilitating Jewish unity—on Purim and throughout the year.

Passover: Freedom, Free Will, and Responsibility

A Longing for Freedom

Of our myriad drives and desires, yearnings, and inclinations, few are as passionate and compelling as the drive for freedom. Freedom is a state of mind. Even more, it is a state of being so essential to human existence that without it the fabric of our lives is bereft of quality, color, and texture.

Children instinctively chase a freedom that is as frightening as it is exciting. Youth defy authority at every turn to pursue the helter-skelter winds of freedom. They don't even know what they will do once they have it—but they know they must have their freedom. Adults too, still yearning and longing, often bolt from the confines of career and family—all for freedom.

Thinkers from every discipline ponder and probe the meaning of freedom. Leaders call upon its power to inspire, and masses rise up to fight and die for it. And finally, there is America, that ennobled bearer of a torch held high to the huddled masses. At its idyllic best, she serves as a humble beacon for all mankind, the land of the free and the home of the brave.

What Is Freedom?

Freedom is the capacity to express in one's life those values and ideals that stem from the essence of the human soul.

The Talmud says, "Precious is the human being who was created in the image of God. And an even greater sign of this preciousness is that man was informed that he was created in God's image." That all human beings are created in the image of God does not mean that there is a bit of Aphrodite and Adonis in all of us but that we all have free will. All human beings possess the ability to make meaningful and substantive choices that have a direct impact on their lives, as well as on the lives of others. It is these choices that determine the ultimate moral and spiritual quality of every human being's existence.

Free Will and Responsibility

Everyone knows that people have the ability to make choices. If you ever did something wrong—and later regretted it—then you believe you had a choice. If you ever felt that a criminal deserved to be punished—despite the socioeconomic factors he was subjected to—then you believe in free will. If you believe that Raoul Wallenberg was a noble and righteous human being, then it's because you believe that he made a choice where so many others failed. And if you ever yell at your kids for leaving their rooms a mess, then you most definitely believe in free will. What you do not believe is that people are bound by the fatalistic chains of familial circumstance, socioeconomic condition, genes, or divine predestination. Thus, you are not prisoner to an attitude of indifference, resignation, and melancholy. Instead you are animated by an abundantly optimistic outlook, which sees yourself and others as shapers, creators, and captains of great ships of potential.

You believe—as Judaism asserts—that people are people and not psychological robots. That the existence of free will automatically creates human responsibility. And that the most precious gift a person can receive is the freedom to make his own choices and to be responsible for his own actions.

Shavuot: It's All about Preparation

The Time of the Giving of our Torah

In the Shavuot prayers, we acknowledge the personality of the holiday with the words *z'man matan torateynu*, "the time of the giving of our Torah." The emphasis here is on the giving of the Torah. In Hebrew, the word for "giving," *matan*, is also the word for "a gift," *matana*. The perspective this wording asks us to consider is twofold. The focus is firstly on God, the giver, and secondly on the fact that what He gave us—the Torah—is a gift.

On Shavuot, God is the active party, so to speak, and our job is to be receptive to His gift. As we have seen, there aren't any special *mitzvot* that we are supposed to do on Shavuot. We don't do anything other than sit back, wait for God to present us with His gift, and then accept it.

There is one little catch to all this, however. This gift of the Torah requires some preparation in order for us to be capable of accepting and holding on to it. In that sense, it's more like an academic university scholarship than a plain old birthday present. Universities offer scholarships not only to students who have proven scholastic abilities but also to those who demonstrate that they will genuinely value the opportunity and will be motivated to make the most out of their gift. To offer a full academic scholarship to someone who is loaded with intelligence and ability but doesn't appreciate the value of higher education is simply a waste.

Now we can more fully understand the riddle of this holiday's name. The Hebrew word *shavuot* means "weeks." This is a reference to the seven weeks that begin with Passover and culminate on Shavuot. Isn't it curious, though, that a holiday would be named after what takes place before it instead of what actually takes place on it? The answer to this riddle is that, from our perspective, Shavuot can be fully meaningful only if the time that precedes it is meaningful. There isn't much to do on Shavuot because the essence of Shavuot lies in the realm of preparation. We prepare to accept God's gift of the Torah so that on Shavuot He can give it to us.

The curious name of the holiday tips us off to the fact that, if we are to access the rich spiritual opportunities that exist within Shavuot, then we must pay close attention to the time that precedes the holiday. The nature of preparation for Shavuot is attitudinal. It's about how we view the gift.

We will now examine three of the essential factors of Shavuot preparations.

1. It's a Gift

If the Torah is a gift, then the question is, How does this inform and guide our preparation? The answer lies in the following perspective:

To view the Torah as a gift means that, in essence, it is for us. For example, when I buy my daughter a new bicycle or computer, it's for her, not for me. It's for her pleasure, not mine; for her good, not mine. I give her gifts because I love her, not myself. The same is true with the Torah. That the Torah is a gift implies that it's for us; it's for our pleasure, our good. It is meant to facilitate our success in life, our achievement of meaning.

Think about it. If the Torah's instructions include a *mitzva* to be sensitive to the needs and feelings of a widow or an orphan, then who are our acts of empathy and kindness for? Are they for us, for God, or for the widow and orphan? Clearly they are for the beneficiaries of our kind deeds, because they are the ones in need. It can also be said that when we go out of our way to assist others, these acts are also for us, because we need to learn to be more sensitive, responsive, and giving. But what about God? Does He need us to be sensitive? Certainly not, because God has no needs. God is complete and perfect in and of Himself. As such, He lacks nothing, has no deficiencies, and therefore doesn't gain anything when we are kind to one another. The same is true with giving charity, fasting on Yom Kippur, eating matzah, and not spreading gossip about people—everything the Torah asks us to do is for us, not God.

In truth, this perspective of "giftness" is the bedrock of all spirituality. Ultimate spirituality is found in a relationship with God, the transcendental source of all, and that relationship begins with a gift.

2. Days Count

We're fairly used to life the way it is, but imagine if our situation were a little different. Imagine if we were born knowing exactly how long we would live, right down to the last minute on the last day of our lives. Do you think we would look at life differently? How about every day of our lives? Certainly as the final months of life ticked away, we would begin to relate to our allotted time a little differently than we would otherwise.

"One day in San Francisco, a dentist friend, while working on my teeth, told me that it was his fiftieth birthday. 'Well then, just ten more years to live, to really live!' I joked through the nitrous oxide. Knowing his delight in physical sport, I floated the possibility that his body might have only another ten years of the energy and stamina necessary for his favorite endeavors, backpacking and wild-river rafting. Though I was only half-kidding, and fifty-five years old myself at the time, he was apparently ripe to hear this, and a few months later changed his office hours to a four-day week, finalized his divorce, and bought a new pair of skis. I have never seen him so lighthearted as when he speaks about how much more time he has to live by giving himself one extra day each week."

Stephen Levine, *A Year to Live* [8]

"Now Abraham was quite old, he came with his days, and God blessed him in every way."

Genesis 24:1

"Now these were the days of the years of the life lived by Abraham, one hundred years and seventy years and five years."

Genesis 25:7

When reflecting on the life of Abraham, founder of the Jewish people, the Torah makes a point of highlighting the days of his life. Here was a man who was aware of his days, made each of them count, and launched the Jewish presence on the stage of history. Four hundred years after the passing of Abraham, his descendants were liberated from Egyptian bondage; forty-nine days later they received the Torah. From that time forth, the Jewish people would commemorate the holiday of Shavuot by counting the forty-nine days that precede the holiday. This path of counting that returns all Jews to the foot of Mount Sinai is known as the *sefira*, the counting period.

To Abraham, every day of life possessed great value, meaning, and potential. Abraham's attitude toward the days of his life belied an all-encompassing love and value for life itself.

The Torah is for people who have a deep regard for days, a deep regard for life.

When we count the days leading to Shavuot, it's not a "countdown" (we don't count from forty-nine backwards until we get to one); rather, we count up. The first day of the *sefira* counting period is day one, the second day is day two, and so forth all the way until day forty-nine.

Some people collect seashells, others collect antiques—Jews collect days. An essential prerequisite to Shavuot is striving to become a collector of days. To cherish not only life, but days. To embrace each day as a fresh opportunity for achievement, for meaning, for growth—for connection to God. After all, isn't that what really counts?

3. A Goal, a Direction, a Purpose

We take for granted that people need goals in life, something to strive for.

We take for granted that people without any sense of direction in life, people who see life as an aimless meandering path to nowhere, are in deep trouble.

We take for granted that the difference between a person who lives with a sense of purpose and one who feels that he has no purpose at all is greater than the difference between night and day.

> *"A powerful way to conceive of the cognitive, cultural, and even, in part, the political life of a society is as a conversation. All we know of social reality is taken from the stream of unending conversations, which constitute it. How could it be otherwise, since people never hear or learn anything else? With the exception of a few strikingly original people, individuals view the world in a manner that is in consonance with their society's conversation."*

Daniel Jonah Goldhagen, *Hitler's Willing Executioners* [9]

We live in a society, a global society, whose conversation is built on the foundation of notions like purpose and goals and direction; on concepts like striving to better oneself and the world one lives in; on dreaming—even attempting—to forge a brighter future for the generations that will inherit the world we leave behind.

It is almost impossible for us to imagine a society devoid of these ideas. If we were asked to conceive of people living not just without a sense of purpose but without even the concept of purpose, we would imagine some Borg-like race of aliens devoid of heart and soul.

Yet, once upon a time, that is precisely what mankind's conversation was like.

> *"All evidence points to there having been, in the earliest religious thought, a vision of the cosmos that was profoundly cyclical. The assumptions that early man made about the world were, in all their essentials, little different in their assumptions that later and more sophis-ticated societies, like Greece and India, would make in a more elaborate manner. As Henri-Charles Puech says of Greek thought in his seminal Man and Time: 'No event is unique, nothing is enacted but once...every event has been enacted, is enacted and will be enacted perpetually; the same individuals have appeared, appear and will appear at every turn of the circle.'"*
>
> Thomas Cahill, *The Gifts of the Jews* [10]

In the ancient world, people saw all of history as nothing more than one big Broadway theatre and all of human life as nothing more than playing one role or another in Broadway's longest-running production. Whether you were an actress playing Grizabella in the original cast of *Cats* or Grizabella in a high school production, your lines were still the same, your part the same, and your future the same. You were just going through the same motions that countless others before you had gone through, uttering the same words that many more would echo after you.

"If we had lived in the second millennium BC, the millennium of Avram (Abraham), and could have canvassed all the nations of the earth,...On every continent, in every society, Avram (Abraham) would have been given the same advice that wise men as diverse as Heraclitus, Lao-Tsu and Siddhartha would one day give their followers: do not journey but sit; compose yourself by the river of life, meditate on its ceaseless and meaningless flow—on all that is past or passing or to come—until you have absorbed the pattern and have come to peace with the Great Wheel and with your own death and the death of all things..."

Thomas Cahill, *The Gifts of the Jews* [11]

The Jewish nation left Egypt and headed out into the wilderness. But this was not a people without a purpose or a goal or a mission. This was a people who knew that, despite hundreds of years of brutal oppression, one day their situation would be different. This was a people who saw a mountain called Sinai not as just another resting place in the wilderness but as an ideal to strive for, as the embodiment of a mission to whose calling they would have to rise.

In Egypt, the Jews were subjected not only to backbreaking labor but also to spirit-breaking labor. They were ordered to build cities on unstable ground only to watch the product of their efforts crumble and then have to start the same work all over again. But this was a people who carried an ancient promise, a promise that, one day, not only would they be free *from*, but they would be free *to*. For forty-nine days the Jewish people traveled, not just away from Egypt but to Mount Sinai. With each passing day, they moved closer and closer to their goal. But even more, with each passing day, they reaffirmed their belief that life could have a goal. That life didn't have to remain the way it had always been. That one doesn't have to be a prisoner of one's past. That there is no script called fate and that, in fact, the scenes of a much brighter future are waiting to be written.

The Torah that we received at Mount Sinai is nothing less than a revolutionary manifesto for changing the world. Our people have the great task of teaching humanity that we have just begun to scratch the surface of human greatness. In biomedicine and molecular physics, as in so many other fields, we are just beginning to realize that while we have come so far, there is still much farther to go. In the realms of morality, spirituality, human dignity, and human consciousness the same is true.

> *"The Jews started it all—and by "it" I mean so many of the things we care about, the underlying values that make all of us, Jew and Gentile, believer and atheist, tick. Without the Jews, we would see the world through different eyes...think with a different mind...And we would set a different course for our lives. There is simply no one else remotely like them; theirs is a unique vocation. Indeed, as we shall see, the very idea of a vocation, of a personal destiny, is a Jewish idea."*
>
> Thomas Cahill, *The Gifts of the Jews* [12]

The Torah, our gift from Sinai, is a never-ending call to reach for more and more of our ultimate potential.

So the name of the holiday is Shavuot, "weeks." And the soul of the holiday can be found in the days that precede it, days during which we strive to lift our vision. With each passing day, we look for yet another way to ready ourselves to accept God's gift and to embrace the privilege of being part of a people capable of inspiring the entire world.

The Ninth of Av: Why Are We Still Crying?

We've Had Our Share of Tragedies

When the Jordanians desecrated synagogues in the Old City of Jerusalem or when arsonists firebombed synagogues in California, that was a tragedy. When Jews were slaughtered by

Cossacks in Russia and tortured by doctors in Germany, that was a tragedy. Jewish history has no shortage of tragedies. But the destruction of the Temple was different. While one can never diminish the untold suffering and death that occurred with the conquest of Jerusalem, another dimension to the tragedy made it uniquely devastating.

The destruction of the Temple crippled the Jewish people's ability to have the fullest possible relationship with God.

The Marriage Paradigm

Imagine a couple who are deeply in love and have been married for over fifty years. There is no end to the ways they have learned to express and communicate their love—a look, a note tucked under a pillow, a touch, a gift, a word. Imagine that the husband is relatively shy and quiet in public, but in the privacy of their home, he beautifully expresses the depths of his love. His eloquence and sincerity are treasured by his wife. And then one day, as the result of an illness, he loses his voice forever.

Is that the end of their love, of their relationship? Of course not. But it is the loss of a uniquely wonderful way of expressing that love and for deepening the bond they have shared for so long. Their love will endure and flourish, yet something will always be missing. They will recall the beautiful words that had once been spoken, and they will smile and cry.

This was the Temple in Jerusalem.

The Temple was a very special aspect of the relationship between God and the Jewish people, between God and every Jew. But it was more than unique; it was able to foster an intense spiritual intimacy that can't be achieved in any other way.

So was the loss of the Temple the loss of the relationship? Certainly not. The relationship endures and even thrives. Yet without the Temple, there is always something missing, always a lack of completion. We look back at the martyrs of Jerusalem and the ruins of the Temple. We look right in front of us and see the State of Israel, and we look to the future. And we smile, and we cry.

epilogue

Simple Complexity

It's true that holidays are wonderful occasions for family gatherings whose feelings, and sounds, and smells can forever imprint themselves on one's psyche. It's also true that holidays are links to a grand historical saga—the story of the Jewish nation. And it is also true that the practices, prayers, and customs of the holidays are endlessly rich sources of insight. However, when viewed separately, any one of these perspectives is only a partial and incomplete picture of what the Jewish holidays are actually all about. Just like a watch is more than just the sum of its parts—but rather is an independent and interdependent body so to speak—so too the holidays. Consider the following definition of a social paradigm—

> *"A constellation of concepts, values, perceptions, and practices shared by a community, which forms a particular vision of reality that is the basis of the way the community organizes itself."*

> Fritjof Capra, *The Web of Life* [13]

The Jewish nation is a community that spans continents and millennia and that possesses, as an elemental social paradigm, the annual cycle of holidays. On the plane of the individual, as well as on the collective national plane, the holidays guide, and inform, and inspire Jews along a path to the deepest experiences of connection to self, to soul, to community, to people, to history, and ultimately to God.

As you leave this book, it is my hope that you leave with a new vision. A vision that, while it is aware of, understands, and even cherishes all the elements that comprise the holidays, no longer sees the holidays as detached fragments of one's Jewish identity. Instead, I hope that you can now begin to see the holidays for what they are: an elegant system for nourishing the Jewish soul.

Chag someach—may you have only joy-filled holidays.

NOTES

1. Johnson, Paul. 1987. *A History of the Jews*. New York: Harper & Row.
2. Grant, Michael. 1991. *The Founders of the Western World*. New York: Scribner.
3. Hawking, Stephen. 1988. *A Brief History of Time*. New York: Bantam Books.
4. Greene, Brian. 1999. *The Elegant Universe*. New York: Vintage Books.
5. Berzovski, Shalom Noach. *Paths of Peace*.
6. Durant, Will. 1963. *Our Oriental Heritage*. New York: Simon and Schuster.
7. Sharansky, Natan. 1/12/2001. Jerusalem Post.
8. Levine, Steve. 1997. *A Year to Live*. New York: Bell Tower Books.
9. Goldhagen, Daniel Jonah. 1996. *Hitler's Willing Executioners*. New York: Alfred A. Knopf.
10. Cahill, Thomas. 1998. *The Gifts of the Jews*. New York: Nan A. Talese.
11. ibid.
12. ibid.
13. Capra, Fritjof. 1996. *The Web of Life*. New York: Anchor Books.

ABOUT THE AUTHOR

Shimon Apisdorf is an award-winning author whose books have been read by hundreds of thousands of people around the world. He has gained a world-wide reputation for his ability to extract the essence of classical Jewish wisdom and show how it can be relevant to issues facing the mind, heart and soul in today's world. Shimon grew up in Cleveland, Ohio, and studied at the University of Cincinnati, Telshe Yeshiva of Cleveland and the Aish HaTorah College of Jewish Studies in Jerusalem. He currently resides with his wife, Miriam, and their children in Baltimore. The Apisdorfs enjoy taking long walks, listening to the music of Sam Glaser and going to Orioles games.

Shimon can be reached at sjapisdorf@earthlink.net

Enjoyed Judaism in a Nutshell?

Other books by Shimon Apisdorf, available at better booksellers or by calling 1-800-LEVIATHAN (538-4284). You can also order online at www.leviathanpress.com.

JUDAISM IN A NUTSHELL: GOD
by Shimon Apisdorf

ROSH HASHANAH YOM KIPPUR SURVIVAL KIT
by Shimon Apisdorf   1993 Benjamin Franklin Award

PASSOVER SURVIVAL KIT   SURVIVAL KIT FAMILY HAGGADAH
by Shimon Apisdorf   by Shimon Apisdorf

CHANUKAH: *EIGHT NIGHTS OF LIGHT, EIGHT GIFTS FOR THE SOUL*
by Shimon Apisdorf   1997 Benjamin Franklin Award

DEATH OF CUPID   ONE HOUR PURIM PRIMER
by Nachum Braverman   by Shimon Apisdorf
and Shimon Apisdorf

THE BIBLE FOR THE CLUELESS BUT CURIOUS
by Nachum Braverman 1997 Benjamin Franklin Award

MISSILES MASKS AND MIRACLES   REMEMBER MY SOUL
by Charles Samuel   by Lori Palatnik